LATE FLOWERING

A Comedy by

JOHN CHAPMAN
and
IAN DAVIDSON

SAMUEL FRENCH, INC.
45 WEST 25TH STREET   NEW YORK 10010
7623 SUNSET BOULEVARD HOLLYWOOD 90046
LONDON   TORONTO

IMPORTANT BILLING AND CREDIT REQUIREMENTS

All producers of LATE FLOWERING *must* give credit to the Author of the Play in all programs distributed in connection with performances of the Play and in all instances in which the title of the Play appears for purposes of advertising, publicizing or otherwise exploiting the Play and/or a production. The name of the Author *must* also appear on a separate line, on which no other name appears, immediately following the title, and *must* appear in size of type not less than fifty percent the size of the title type.

CHARACTERS
(in order of appearance)

DAPHNE PARDOE
ELIZABETH FOSTER-BULLER
CONSTANCE BEAUMONT
MARTIN WHITTAKER
CAROLINE PINDER

═══════════════════════════

ACT I	Scene 1	A morning in May
ACT I	Scene 2	The following morning
ACT II	Scene 1	The same, three weeks later
ACT II	Scene 2	That evening
ACT II	Scene 3	The next day

ACT I

Scene 1

(The play is set in the spacious Reception Room of the Beaumont Marriage Bureau, just off Sloane Square. The room is on the first floor of an Edwardian mansion block, and has long double windows Stage R.

Upstage C is the main door onto the landing and mid-way down the L wall is a door leading to an apartment where the owner, CONSTANCE BEAUMONT lives.

The furnishings have an air of slightly faded splendor. The walls are panelled. There is a knee-hole desk below the window on which are a typewriter and a box file.

On the opposite side of the room there is a large knee-hole desk with a vase of flowers, a pen-set and a blotter.

Center Stage there is a Chesterfield and a coffee table with magazines and more flowers. A leather wing-back chair stands behind the big desk. The curtains and cushions are floral and the general impression is one of femininity, not a gentleman's Club.

As the curtain rises the center door opens and DAPHNE PARDOE enters. She is the loyal, hard-working secretary of the Beaumont Bureau. A woman in her mid-fifties. She goes to her desk, D.R. puts some letters on the desk and opens a drawer, puts her hand in and switches on the an-

*swering machine. She then goes out again into the landing
and returns with a four feet high folding screen in a taste-
ful brocade. She erects it around the computer in order to
hide it. As she does this the "Answering Machine" begins
to replay its messages.)*

MAN's VOICE ON MACHINE. Oh, hello—er—I've never
actually—er—well no I think perhaps I won't—

(The Machine bleeps.)

WOMAN's VOICE ON MACHINE. I wonder if you
could—er—sometime in the near future—well no, doesn't
matter.

(The Machine bleeps.)

WOMAN's VOICE ON MACHINE. Ah yes, perhaps you
can ring me back if I just give you my name—*(DAPHNE lis-
tens attentively while she takes off her coat and hangs it up.)*
It's er—no p'raps not.

(The Machine bleeps.)

MAN's BUSINESSLIKE VOICE. Good morning. I haven't
got much time, but just let me say I haven't ever approached a
Marriage Bureau before, after all it's not the sort of thing one
does every day of one's life, but now I've made up my mind
to do it, I hope the whole thing can be done quickly and with
the minimum of fuss. So I'll just give you my name and address. *(DAPHNE dashes to the desk and picks up her pen.)*
No, sorry, thought better of it. Some other time.

*(DAPHNE switches off the machine and closes the drawer.
She sits at the desk and starts to open a letter and the telephone rings. DAPHNE lifts the receiver.)*

DAPHNE. Good morning, the Beaumont Bureau, can I help you?—Oh yes, I remember you Mr. Summers, forty-two, clean-shaven, five foot eleven, fly fishing. C of E.—yes, did you meet Miss Pinder?—oh dear—oh dear—oh dear, oh dear—yes you would be—well these things happen. Would you like Miss Beaumont to ring you later?—Right, good-bye. *(She replaces the telephone.)* Oh dear. *(She rifles through her filing box.)* Pinder, Pinder. *(She takes out a card, puts a cross on it and returns it to the box, as the door bell rings.)* Come in.

(The door opens and an intense lady enters. She is in her late forties. She is MRS. FOSTER-BULLER.)

MRS. FOSTER-BULLER. Is there any news from Mr. Thurston?

DAPHNE. Ah—well—er—

MRS. FOSTER-BULLER. Where are the man's manners? It's been three weeks and his last words were—"we must do this again." I mean what does that mean to you?

DAPHNE. Well—

MRS. FOSTER-BULLER. It sounds like an invitation to me, but have I received any details of the time and the place? Four thirty at Fortnum & Masons Soda Fountain. Three o'clock the Sainsbury Wing of the National Gallery. Six thirty under a clock somewhere? Well have I?

DAPHNE. When you put it like that—er—

MRS. FOSTER-BULLER. Henry would never have treated me like that Henry was punctilious to a fault. Where's Miss Beaumont?

DAPHNE. She's not here yet.

MRS. FOSTER-BULLER. But I though she lived on the premises.

(MRS. FOSTER-BULLER goes towards the door L.)

DAPHNE. *(Hastily heading her off.)* She doesn't come through into the office until ten.

MRS. FOSTER-BULLER. It's gone ten.

DAPHNE. Only just.

MRS. FOSTER-BULLER. I'm not going until I've seen her.

DAPHNE. Of course not. Do sit down Mrs. Foster-Buller. Would you like a magazine?

MRS. FOSTER-BULLER. Are these the same curtains?

DAPHNE. Do you mean is this one the same as that one?

MRS. FOSTER-BULLER. No, I mean are they the same as the ones before.

DAPHNE. Yes.

MRS. FOSTER-BULLER. Don't let it be too long before you have them cleaned. I wanted to do ours at the Rectory, before Henry died. They were covered in dust, no good for him at all. I took them down and they disintegrated.

DAPHNE. Oh dear.

(DAPHNE is opening the mail.)

MRS. FOSTER-BULLER. Into a thousand pieces.

DAPHNE. Oh dear.

MRS. FOSTER-BULLER. All over the carpet.

DAPHNE. Oh dear, oh dear.

MRS. FOSTER-BULLER. We'd had them all our married life but they don't last for ever do they?

DAPHNE. Twenty-one years.

MRS. FOSTER-BULLER. Twenty something.

DAPHNE. Twenty one.

MRS. FOSTER-BULLER. Did I ever tell you I *didn't* get Henry through Miss Beaumont?

DAPHNE. Yes, I think you did.

MRS. FOSTER-BULLER. *(Not listening.)* I suppose you were doing your best but you sent me out with the most dreary succession of men. So there I was, on a Tuesday in June, sitting next to some chinless wonder from your files—and on the other side of me was this gorgeous man—Adonis in Holy Orders. I couldn't take my eyes off him. Both our hands went to put the sixpence in the binocular slot at the same time. They touched. And that was it.

(MRS. FOSTER-BULLER sighs.)

DAPHNE. Do you tell everybody that story?
MRS. FOSTER-BULLER. Oh yes.
DAPHNE. Mr. thurston as well?
MRS. FOSTER-BULLER. Certainly.
DAPHNE. That could be why you haven't heard from him.
MRS. FOSTER-BULLER. Oh surely not.
DAPHNE. I can't help. We don't want to waste your money.
MRS. FOSTER-BULLER. I wonder you have the gall to bring up money. I should have had a rebate last time. It was me that found Henry for myself.
DAPHNE. Only because you were dating through our agency.
MRS. FOSTER-BULLER. Oh don't uses that dreadful word. "Meeting", "Rendez-vous", not *dating*. I should've had a refund.
DAPHNE. The Beaumont Agency only returns money in the most extreme circumstances.
MRS. FOSTER-BULLER. Well, this wretched Thurston man failing to contact me—that's extreme circumstances. I shall wait here and have it out with Miss Beaumont. I shall tell Miss Beaumont—*(At this point, the door stage L opens and CONSTANCE BEAUMONT enters, dressed smartly for the day's work and carrying a cup of coffee. She takes two paces into the room, sees MRS. FOSTER-BULLER, then tries to tiptoe backwards slowly toward the door.)*—that unless I can get some sort of satisfaction from this man I shall—*(Spotting CONSTANCE as she almost gets out of the door.)*—Ah! Miss Beaumont, there you are.

(CONSTANCE with a charming smile moves into forward gear.)

CONSTANCE. Ah! Mrs. Foster-Buller, good morning.

MRS. FOSTER-BULLER. I've been talking to Miss Pardoe about the dreadful Thurston man. Not so much as a letter or a 'phone call in three weeks. Would it take you three weeks to decide whether to invite me out again?

CONSTANCE. No it wouldn't. I would know immediately. But you know what men are like—*(Quick as a flash.) apart from* Henry, that is!!

MRS. FOSTER-BULLER. Ah Henry. If all men were like Henry, you'd be out of business, Miss Beaumont.

CONSTANCE. Have you come up form Reading this morning?

MRS. FOSTER-BULLER. I bought a monthly season ticket on the strength of Mr. Thurston. A waste of money that's been. It expires next Tuesday.

CONSTANCE. I'll contact Mr. Thurston. Why don't you go off and do your shopping? Have a spot of lunch and come back this afternoon?

MRS. FOSTER-BULLER. Tell him Henry would never have behaved in such an off-hand manner.

CONSTANCE. I won't be mentioning Henry at all.

MRS. FOSTER-BULLER *(Not listening.)* I want a time and a place.

CONSTANCE. I'll tell him.

MRS. FOSTER-BULLER. Don't let him wriggle out of it.

CONSTANCE. I can be very firm.

MRS. FOSTER-BULLER. And if it's the Albert Hall, tell him not by door "16". That's where I always met Henry.

CONSTANCE. Good-bye Mrs. Foster-Buller. *(She finally gets MRS. FOSTER-BULLER out of the door and closes it.)* We could always call it a day and give her her money back I suppose.

DAPHNE. If you start returning money to awkward clients, you'll go out of business. Anyway, you've no need to ring up Mr. Thurston. There's a letter from him.

(DAPHNE passes the letter to CONSTANCE.)

CONSTANCE. Why didn't you tell Mrs. Foster-Buller?
DAPHNE. Why do you think?
CONSTANCE. *(Reads out letter.)* "Dear Miss Beaumont. Sorry so long out of contact but April v. busy month in garden. Also still reeling from encounter with Buller woman. Takes all sorts I suppose, but strikes me Henry took easy way out poor—bastard crossed out—sod. Nil Desperandum. Yours still in hope. J.A. Thurston." I refuse to admit defeat with either of them. This is just the sort of problem we got the computer for. Everything's on that computer. *(She glances in the direction of the computer and stops.)* What's that screen thing doing there?
DAPHNE. The Collisons are coming for a drink this evening. You hadn't forgotten?
CONSTANCE. Ah the Collisons. How could I forget? My first success. They've been married twenty years today.
DAPHNE. Yes and they won't want the green-eyed monster staring at them from the corner of the room.
CONSTANCE. I doubt if they'll even notice it.
DAPHNE. We've got a lovely office here and that thing looks like something out of "Startrek".
CONSTANCE. Nonsense, you're just old-fashioned.
DAPHNE. I think I must be allergic to the Twentieth Century.
CONSTANCE. Well you've left it a little late Daphne dear, it's almost the Twenty-first. And like it or not, one must move with the times.
DAPHNE. We don't need a computer. I've got my filing system. And what isn't on these cards is in here.

(DAPHNE taps her head.)

CONSTANCE. Daphne, those grubby little cards of yours are holding us back. Everytime a client sees them I almost die of shame.

DAPHNE. They were good enough for your Aunt.

CONSTANCE. But some of them are so thumbed and dog-eared.

DAPHNE. They're the clients who've been taken out a lot.

CONSTANCE. You make us sound like a public library. And it's such a give-away when you take out an old card. Any Client who sees it assumes they're being given someone who's been on our books for years and passed through many hands.

DAPHNE. I always replace them when they get too old.

CONSTANCE. And what happens if, God forbid, you get run over by a bus. Only you understand your little hieroglyphics—*(Picking out a grubby one)*. "TW-YR-BAR BK-BK-DVD, One D. Three S."

DAPHNE. Twelve years in Barclays Bank, Bangkok. Divorced. One daughter and three sons.

CONSTANCE. MKT H'BUG?

DAPHNE. Market Harborough.

CONSTANCE. And R.C. Roman Catholic?

DAPHNE. Ruddy complexion.

CONSTANCE. You see? I'd be wasting my time matching an R.C. with an R.C. wouldn't I?

DAPHNE. Well in some cases, R.C. does mean R.C.

CONSTANCE. When?

DAPHNE. When they're pasty-faced. Look, if you're really worried about my cards, I could type them all out in full.

CONSTANCE. Fine. Straight onto the computer.

DAPHNE. I cannot work the computer.

CONSTANCE. You've got the instruction book.

DAPHNE. Yes, but you need an instruction book to explain the instruction book.

CONSTANCE. You have to allow for the fact that it's a

translation from the Japanese.

DAPHNE. My young nephew owns a Japanese car. It's called a "Charade". Now I ask you, who in their right mind would choose that name for a car. I assume it's a direct translation of the Japanese word for "Charade". And that's exactly what the instruction book is—a charade.

CONSTANCE. Then it's a jolly good job I've got a man coming to explain it to you this morning.

DAPHNE. I shall be out.

CONSTANCE. Daphne you're becoming irrational. I haven't seen you as het up as this since the Snowdons separated.

DAPHNE. The Palace should never have allowed the marriage in the first place. If they'd come to me, I'd've given chapter and verse—

CONSTANCE. Yes, Daphne, yes, so you always say. But the Beaumont Bureau wasn't involved, so they didn't.

DAPHNE. In those days we did handle the odd Royal— Continental mostly of course, Royal with a small "R".

CONSTANCE. We certainly haven't had any since I took over, nor have we had many of the aristocracy, they're getting rather thin on the ground.

DAPHNE. Everybody's getting thin on the ground—people aren't getting married like they used to—

CONSTANCE. Then we have to try harder using modern technology. So that when people do come through the door we look as if we're part of the Nineteen "nineties," not like some Dickensian counting-house.

(CONSTANCE has removed the screen and switches on the computer.)

DAPHNE. These simple files were started by your Aunt when she established the—*(The telephone rings.)* Good morning, Beaumont Bureau. Oh, Mr. Summers, I'm sorry. She was just about to ring you. Hold on—*(She covers the mouthpiece, speaks to CONSTANCE.)* Mr. Summers! Big problem with Miss Pinder.

(CONSTANCE moves to her desk and takes the call.)

CONSTANCE. *(Sympathetic.)* Oh Mr. Summers—tell me all—She didn't?—She did?—She didn't?—She did—*did* she? Well I think we must put it down to nerves. It sounds like nerves to me ... Yes it may have looked like Babycham but it *sounds* like nerves. And the heat, and the excitement, well, of meeting you, of course. It's not every day of the week Miss Pinder meets a—

DAPHNE. *(Prompting.)* Five foot eleven. Forty-two, fly-fishing, C of E.

CONSTANCE. It's not every day she meet a fine figure of a young Anglican angler—how long did you have to wait outside the Ladies?—Oh she'd fallen asleep—well I wasn't aware of any little weaknesses when I interview her, but never mind, even as we speak Miss Pardoe is running you through the computer again.

DAPHNE. No she's not!

CONSTANCE. We'll be in touch, good-bye.

(CONSTANCE quickly replaces the receiver.)

DAPHNE. I've already come up with three names. You tell me a computer that's as fast as that.

CONSTANCE. *(Reading the list.)* Marigold Sparks—possible. Diana Crewe—at a pinch. Amanda Wimperis—Dear God, Daphne, are you mad? She's anti-blood sports, he's a fly-fisherman.

DAPHNE. She doesn't have to go with him when he's fishing.

CONSTANCE. And another thing, he's C of E. and she's an atheist.

DAPHNE. One might convert the other.

CONSTANCE. He needn't convert her. Half the Synod are atheists. No, I'll put my money on Diana Crewe. Thirty-eight, divorced, no children, good-looking, in a heavy sort of way.

DAPHNE. Also a heavy smoker.

CONSTANCE. Poor Mr. Summers. He doesn't have a lot of luck. Still—nobody falls asleep in the Ladies from smoking. *(The doorbell rings.)* Come in!

(A man's head appears round the door. It belongs to MARTIN WHITTAKER. A bit of a "brain-box" with computers but very unworldly otherwise.)

MARTIN. Beaumont Bureau?

CONSTANCE. Yes.

MARTIN Ten o'clock Wednesday?

CONSTANCE. Yes.

MARTIN. You're expecting someone from Sincomat?

CONSTANCE. About our computer?

MARTIN. *(Stepping in.)* Then this must be it. No mistakes so far. *(Looks round admiring the room.)* I don't see many offices like this nowadays. Delightful. You've got a lot of old world charm. *(Hastily.)* Not you personally, because I don't know you. But you might have. Now which one of you am I talking to?

CONSTANCE. *(Puzzled.)* Me, aren't you?

MARTIN. Ah, then you're Miss Beaumont.

CONSTANCE. Yes, and this is Miss Pardoe, my secretary.

MARTIN. How do you do? *(Shakes hands with both ladies.)* My name's Whittaker, Martin Whittaker.

CONSTANCE. Would you like a coffee?

MARTIN. *(Sees the machine.)* Ah! A Mitsoka 2000 S.L. And if I'm not mistaken with a "Modem" and a "Hard-drive.". Am I right?

CONSTANCE. Very possibly.

MARTIN. Good. Well if I'm any judge it'll be the "blitter-chip". *(He undoes his briefcase and takes out a screw-driver.)*

They up-graded these to 4 megabytes and it wasn't a good idea. Not in my opinion. *(He starts to unscrew the back of the computer.)* I mean, it can't handle peripherals, but there's no denying you get a lovely "WYSIWYG"— (Wissywig.)

CONSTANCE. A what?

MARTIN. Wissywig.

CONSTANCE. Oh, Wissywig.

MARTIN. Oh yes, a lovely one. *(Turns to DAPHNE with a chuckle.)* I've an idea your boss doesn't know what "WYSIWYG" is.

DAPHNE. Neither of us knows and I'm happy in my ignorance.

MARTIN. Oh dear, oh dear. Perhaps I will have that coffee.

CONSTANCE. After you've told us what this fascinating word means.

MARTIN. *(Spells it out.)* W-Y-S-I-W-Y-G. It stands for "What You See Is What You Get."

CONSTANCE. Now isn't that interesting Daphne?

DAPHNE. No.

CONSTANCE. Get Mr. Whittaker a coffee.

DAPHNE. How do you like it?

MARTIN. As it comes.

DAPHNE. Black? White? Sugar? No sugar?

MARTIN. Why not?

CONSTANCE. You must have a preference Mr. Whittaker.

MARTIN. It's only a hot drink after all.

DAPHNE. Ah, hot? Well that's something to hang on to.

(DAPHNE exits L. MARTIN continues to take the back off.)

CONSTANCE. Do you have to take it apart?

MARTIN. Got to get a move on. I was ten minutes late arriving, in the office that is—I mean I was circling Sloane Square twenty minutes ago, but not a hope of parking, no chance. But then saw one of those lorries with a crane thing on the back, I thought—"Ah"—so I followed it, they hoiked a car out, and I was in.

CONSTANCE. Not for long, I wouldn't have thought.

MARTIN. Forty minutes. They've got to get to Camberwell and back. Where do you park every day?

CONSTANCE. I don't have that problem. I live on the premises.

MARTIN. You mean this room converts?

CONSTANCE. No. I live through there and Miss Pardoe walks to work.

MARTIN. How very handy. I wish I could walk to work. (Looks at his watch.) If I don't get this computer fixed in thirty minutes, I could be walking home.

CONSTANCE. I'm not sure you have to take it apart.

MARTIN. It says on my docket that the machine doesn't work.

CONSTANCE. No, well it doesn't work, but to be precise it doesn't work for Daphne.

MARTIN. Oh I see. *(Puts his screw-driver away.)* She has trouble with instructions perhaps.

CONSTANCE. She has trouble with mine certainly.

MARTIN. I meant the instructions that come with the hardware.

CONSTANCE. *(Lost.)* Hardware?

MARTIN. Yes, hardware. Bless my soul, it's back to basics with you, isn't it? The machine is the hardware and the programme is the software. I'll just slip one in and see if it's working.

(MARTIN takes one from his case and taps away as DAPHNE returns with a cup and saucer and a cafe filter on a tray.)

CONSTANCE. Ah, what a delightful sound. The gentle clicking, it's like listening to some Chinese people playing Mahjong.

(It now becomes a "Shoot 'em up" game with loud electronic music.)

DAPHNE. And even the Boxer Rebellion.

CONSTANCE. Mr. Whittaker please—*(The noise continues.)* Mr. Whittaker! Your coffee!

MARTIN. Oh yes, thank you.

CONSTANCE. Do you think you could turn the volume down?

MARTIN. Certainly. *(He does so.)* Absolutely nothing wrong with the machine.

CONSTANCE. Thank you.

MARTIN. *(Takes a sip of coffee.)* Ow!!

DAPHNE. Careful.

MARTIN. It's hot.

DAPHNE. You're a difficult man to cater for Mr. Whittaker.

(MARTIN sucks in coffee and air—making a loud noise.)

CONSTANCE. Are you married Mr. Whittaker?

MARTIN. No.

CONSTANCE. I thought not. No woman would tolerate the way you drink coffee.

MARTIN. I'm sorry. *(He puts coffee aside to let it cool. He turns to DAPHNE.)* I gather you're not too clever with instructions.

DAPHNE. Gather?

CONSTANCE. All I said, Daphne, was that you weren't entirely conversant with the language these things are written in.

MARTIN. It's only the machine that's Japanese, not the instructions.

DAPHNE. They might just as well be.

CONSTANCE. Perhaps they lose something in the translation.

DAPHNE. Yes, me for a start.

MARTIN. *(Turns off the machine and removes the disc.)* I

think you're doing yourself an injustice Miss Pardoe. You're cleverer than you look.

CONSTANCE. Oh she is.

DAPHNE. Thank you.

MARTIN. I can teach you to use your programme in ten minutes. What is it you've got? Word processor—data base—spread sheets?

CONSTANCE. We bought a special programme, so we can compare people's characteristics, and get a perfect match.

MARTIN. *(A pause.)* Organ donors you mean? Kidneys, eye-balls, that sort of thing?

CONSTANCE. No, a match for life, for marriage.

MARTIN. Are you serious.

CONSTANCE. Of course.

DAPHNE. This is a Marriage Bureau.

MARTIN. Good heavens, that explains it!

CONSTANCE. What?

MARTIN. That woman in the red hat in the foyer. I came in, I said—"Am I right for the Beaumont Bureau"? She said—"Stand still a moment," and she looked me up and down as if I was a side of beef.

DAPHNE. Mrs. Foster-Buller.

MARTIN. She walked slowly round me and said—"Henry's seat was always shiny too."

CONSTANCE. Henry was her late husband. This Agency had the pleasure of introducing them to each other.

MARTIN. Ah, I see.

DAPHNE. Henry was a Vicar. He might've been a Dean had he lived.

MARTIN. Man of the cloth—I expect his knees were shiny too—so the woman in the red hat's come back for a refill has she?

CONSTANCE. Refill? This is a highly respectable firm, Mr. Whittaker. Established by my great-aunt in 1923 and has flourished ever since without a breath of scandal or impropriety.

DAPHNE. If you don't count that woman in Cromer.

CONSTANCE. Barring the woman in Cromer.

MARTIN. *(Picking up the disc.)* So what's on this disc? Have you put in any of the names?

(MARTIN puts the disc into the computer, boots it up.)

DAPHNE. I've put in all he names of our Clients. *All* their details, it's full of information, it just won't do anything with it.

CONSTANCE. *(To DAPHNE.)* The first hiccup, you ditched it.

MARTIN. Computers don't have hiccups. They have bugs.

DAPHNE. That's why the instruction might as well be in Japanese. It's full of jargon like 'bugs'. Men love jargon.

MARTIN. As a matter of fact, the word 'bug' was coined by a woman.

DAPHNE. Someone's secretary?

MARTIN. No. She was an American Admiral, Grace Hopper. The first lady of software. They kept her in the U.S. Navy 'til she was eighty. Amazing. Amazing Grace, they called her.

CONSTANCE. I don't believe you. You can't be in the Navy when you're eighty—not even the American Navy.

MARTIN. Oh yes you can. Although they had to pass a special Act of Congress. She invented computer languages. Just like this one. Wonderful woman. *(Then to DAPHNE.)* What is it you find so difficult?

DAPHNE. Oh, it's not that it's difficult. I mean I'm sure I could understand it if I just watched a demonstration.

MARTIN. *(Reads the instruction book.)* This is wrong, they've got it wrong.

DAPHNE. I thought it couldn't be me.

MARTIN. It says—"key in—slash—question mark—dot." It should be round the other way.

DAPHNE. What?

MARTIN. Dot—question mark—slash.

CONSTANCE. You listen hard to what the man's saying.

MARTIN. *(To DAPHNE.)* You sit here. I'll show you. Are you ready?

DAPHNE. Yes.

MARTIN. Key in—"dot—question mark—slash."

DAPHNE. *(Does it.)* Dot—question mark—slash.

MARTIN. There you are. There's your menu.

CONSTANCE. You've never got this far before.

MARTIN. Now you choose what you want to do. Use the mouse.

DAPHNE. The mouse. Oh yes.

(DAPHNE takes hold of the mouse.)

MARTIN. Run it down the menu, click on to what you want.

CONSTANCE. Try Mix and Match.

DAPHNE. *(Does it.)* Oh look, it's all there.

MARTIN. Now just type in what you're looking for. Give it a 'for instance.'

CONSTANCE. See if it'll pick out the non-smoking music lovers with a sense of humor.

(DAPHNE does so.)

MARTIN. Give it a real test. Non-smoking, music lovers, with a sense of humor, under five foot two.

(DAPHNE taps keyboard.)

DAPHNE. It's not working.

MARTIN. You haven't tapped "enter."

DAPHNE. Oh sorry. There.

(DAPHNE taps it.)

MARTIN. *(Types in "Under five feet two and then presses enter.)* Here we are. Miss Josephine Ribbins. Now I'll click onto her name. *(He moves the mouse.)* Press 'escape'. *(He does so.)* And there's her details. Age 32, Ministry of Agriculture and Fisheries. Not interested in country pursuits. What's she doing in the Min. of Ag. and Fish then?

CONSTANCE. Mr. Whittaker, this information is given to us in strict confidence.

MARTIN. *(Reading.)* Non-smoking, non-drinking, vegetarian, hobbies: reading. Dear me.

CONSTANCE. Come away from there.

MARTIN. And under five feet two. I'm not surprised she's been overlooked.

CONSTANCE. We do not make judgments about our Clients Mr. Whittaker and I'd rather you didn't.

MARTIN. But it sort of tears at the heart strings doesn't it? This poor, half-starved, meek little Civil Servant, living a dull life, she's on the shelf, wouldn't you say?

CONSTANCE. 'Shelf' is a word we never use in our profession. Anyone who has signed up with the Beaumont Bureau is not only off the shelf, but half-way up the aisle.

MARTIN. Almost at the 'check-out'.

CONSTANCE. This is not a Cash and Carry, Mr. Whittaker.

MARTIN. It's a rum business though, isn't it? I mean when you come to think of it, there's all these Clients of yours, giving you all these details about themselves. Half of which are probably lies anyway.

CONSTANCE. Lies?!!

MARTIN. Vegetarian, with a sense of humor? I've yet to meet one and I'll bet she eats chicken. And who's going to say "no" to a question like—"Have you got a sense of humor?"

CONSTANCE. They certainly don't tell lies about what they're looking for.

MARTIN. They don't know what they're looking for. And if they did know why haven't they found it for themselves before now?

CONSTANCE. I can help them, Miss Pardoe can help them.

MARTIN. "Miss" Pardoe? What can she know about marriage. Are you married?

CONSTANCE. No.

MARTIN. Well it seems to me the only thing she's qualified to work in this office is that computer.

CONSTANCE. Isn't your car on a double yellow line?

MARTIN. Sugar!! Sorry. Cripes yes.

(MARTIN packs his case quickly.)

CONSTANCE. You'll be sending us a bill will you?

MARTIN. In the fullness of time, yes.

CONSTANCE. I shall question it of course.

MARTIN. Of course. Good-bye Miss Pardoe.

DAPHNE. *(Looking up from her work.)* Oh you're going. Good-bye and thank you for your help.

MARTIN. It was a pleasure, and if you get stuck again, don't hesitate to call me.

(MARTIN goes to the door.)

CONSTANCE. We'll hesitate it we want to. I'm sure there are other computer experts in London.

MARTIN. *(At the door.)* Ah yes, but not with a sense of humor.

(MARTIN exits.)

CONSTANCE. So far, this has been a most dispiriting day Daphne.

DAPHNE. Speaking for myself, I feel quite exhilarated.

CONSTANCE. Oh good, every cloud has a silver lining.

DAPHNE. Is it all right if I go on practising?

CONSTANCE. Only if you can find someone suitable for Mr. Summers. I'm feeling rather sorry for that poor man, and his dreadful experience with Miss Pinder.

DAPHNE. Right. *(Typing.)* Slash—dot—question mark—space bar—click. Ah! *(Typing.)* Summers. *(Presses button.)* "Enter"—here we go—oh dear.

CONSTANCE. Now what?

DAPHNE. It says his ideal partner is Miss Pinder.

CONSTANCE. That's the same mistake that *we* made. Tell it to pull its socks up.

DAPHNE. I don't think there's a knob for that.

CONSTANCE. I'll have to look through your cards. *(She picks them up and takes them to her desk.)* Who would've thought she could let herself down like that. She always struck me as being very demure.

DAPHNE. Still waters run deep.

CONSTANCE. Only in her case it wasn't water.

DAPHNE. I wouldn't like to have her head this morning.

(MISS PINDER has entered through the main door. She wears sunglasses and walks carefully.)

CONSTANCE. Nor I.

DAPHNE. I'd be surprised if she ever shows her face her again.

CONSTANCE. *(Noticing MISS PINDER.)* Look surprised Daphne.

(DAPHNE sees MISS PINDER.)

DAPHNE. Oh Miss Pinder, you look a little delicate.

MISS PINDER. He never waited. When I came out of the Ladies he'd gone.

(CONSTANCE goes to support MISS PINDER.)

CONSTANCE. Yes, but you were in the Ladies for an hour.

MISS PINDER. I only had a little snooze, it was 'flu'.

CONSTANCE. If it's 'flu', you shouldn't be out.

MISS PINDER. It was the twenty-four hour sort. I'm fine now.

CONSTANCE. You don't look it, Daphne, make some more coffee. *(DAPHNE exits L.)* You drank too many Babychams, didn't you?

MISS PINDER. I might have done.

CONSTANCE. *You did.* I've had Mr. Summers on the 'phone, poor man. I expect more of my girls Caroline, you've let the side down.

MISS PINDER. Yes I know. I'm frightfully sorry. It's always been my problem. Two Babychams and I'm nobodys!!

CONSTANCE. You're certainly not Mr. Summers!!

(MISS PINDER bursts into tears.)

MISS PINDER. He was sweet too! He goes fishing. I've always wanted to go fishing with a man, with a moustache.

CONSTANCE. *(She consults the notes over MISS PINDER's back.)* Moustache? He didn't tell us. He's down here as clean-shaven. He'll have to be re-listed.

MISS PINDER. I knew under the clock he was sweet. I never had such a strong feeling before. So I had a Babycham to steady my nerves. And he told me all about fishing.

CONSTANCE. How exciting.

MISS PINDER. *(Nods.)* So I had another Babycham.

CONSTANCE. I wish I had shares in Babycham.

MISS PINDER. I don't even know his 'phone number! He never gave me his 'phone number. I want his 'phone number.

CONSTANCE. I can't give it to you without his consent. I doubt if he wants you to have it.

(Enter DAPHNE with coffee for all.)

DAPHNE. Cheer up, Miss Pinder. Plenty more fish in the sea.

(MISS PINDER bursts out crying.)

CONSTANCE. Try not to mention fish, Daphne, it's a sore point.

DAPHNE. Doesn't she like fish?

CONSTANCE. Mr. Summers is a keen angler. And what's more, he's got himself a moustache from somewhere.

DAPHNE. When did he grow that?

CONSTANCE. I don't know.

DAPHNE. How long does it take men to grow moustaches?

CONSTANCE. I've really no idea.

DAPHNE. He didn't mention it on the 'phone this morning.

(MISS PINDER lets out another wail.)

CONSTANCE. Oh come along Caroline, cheer up.

MISS PINDER. You don't understand.

CONSTANCE. Of course we do.

MISS PINDER. He was just right. By a pure stroke of luck, he was my ideal.

CONSTANCE. Luck doesn't come into it! He's your ideal because the Beaumont Bureau chose him for you. We don't just pull names out of a hat you know.

DAPHNE. And now we have a computer. We'll have to see what other ideal men we can find for you.

MISS PINDER. I don't want any other ideal men! I want Mr. Summers.

CONSTANCE. You should have though of that before you drank yourself under the table.

(MISS PINDER sobs. A ring at the front door bell.)

DAPHNE. Shall I?

(DAPHNE is indicating the door.)

CONSTANCE. No, I will. Just take Miss Pinder out of here. She's not a very good advertisement.

DAPHNE. Come along, this way.

(MISS PINDER is still crying.)

CONSTANCE. And for heaven's sake, keep her quiet. *(The front door bell rings again.)* Coming, coming. *(CONSTANCE opens the door as DAPHNE and MISS PINDER exit L.)* Ah Mrs. Foster-Buller, I thought you went shopping.

MRS. FOSTER-BULLER. *(Entering.)* There was a bomb scare.

CONSTANCE. Oh.

MRS. FOSTER-BULLER. What did Mr. Thurston say?

CONSTANCE. You must brace yourself.

MRS. FOSTER-BULLER. *(Interested.)* Oh why did he say that?

CONSTANCE. He didn't. I'm saying it.

MRS. FOSTER-BULLER. You're not going to tell me he doesn't want to see me.

CONSTANCE. He feels the two of you aren't on the same wave-length.

MRS. FOSTER-BULLER. Wave-length? What does he mean by wave-length? He's not a spiritualist is he?

CONSTANCE. No. C of E. He just means that he feels you're poles apart and both set in your ways.

MRS. FOSTER-BULLER. Well he can change can't he?

CONSTANCE. I don't think so, to be frank I'd say it's a blessing in disguise. Let's face it, Mr. Thurston is not one of the "Henry's" of this world.

MRS. FOSTER-BULLER. There was only one Henry. Sometimes I think he stands beside me, you know.

CONSTANCE. I think that's what Mr. Thurston feels too.

MRS. FOSTER-BULLER. Perhaps you could give me his address ... ?

CONSTANCE. No, no. We never give addresses or telephone numbers, unless specifically instructed by the parties themselves.

MRS. FOSTER-BULLER. Well, not use crying over spilt milk then. I'm here now so ... what's that noise?

CONSTANCE. One of our Clients had a rather unfortunate experience last night.

MRS. FOSTER-BULLER. Oh dear. Sounds like a soul in torment.

CONSTANCE. She missed her opportunity.

MRS. FOSTER-BULLER. Oh—well at least that won't be my epitaph. I took my opportunity. Though I could have taken it earlier. I wasted two years of Henry, you know. He proposed to me in September and I didn't say 'yes' 'til the July nearly two years later. Two years!

(MRS. FOSTER-BULLER begins to weep.)

CONSTANCE. Please ... Mrs. Foster-Buller ...
MRS. FOSTER-BULLER. Two wasted years!

(MRS. FOSTER-BULLER weeps silently, enter DAPHNE leaving the door to CONSTANCE's flat open.)

DAPHNE. She's inconsolable! I'm doing my best but ... could you try?

CONSTANCE. Not now Daphne, we're having a little problem in here as well.

DAPHNE. Oh dear, was it something that happened when she was shopping?

CONSTANCE. She's been thinking about Henry.

MRS. FOSTER-BULLER. I lost something precious!

DAPHNE. I beg your pardon?

MRS. FOSTER-BULLER. Two years of my life!!

CONSTANCE. Rushing into things doesn't always work. Perhaps you needed those two years. Perhaps it all turned out for the best, the way it was. You said your life was idyllic. I've been in this business for ever so many years and you were the first person to use that word to me. Idyllic. Twenty-one idyllic years. How many of us can say that?

MRS. FOSTER-BULLER. Who's to say it wouldn't have been idyllic with Mr. Thurston?

DAPHNE. I think you can only have one idyll, can't you?

CONSTANCE. Unless you're royalty and have the Idylls of the King. Miss Pardoe's right—*(Ring at the door.)* Are we expecting anyone, Daphne?

DAPHNE. Not that I know of. I must go back to that poor girl—

CONSTANCE. Answer the door first. See if you can get rid of them.

(The door opens. MARTIN enters.)

MARTIN. Don't disturb yourselves. It's all right. I can let myself in.

DAPHNE. Mr. Whittaker!

CONSTANCE. What have you come back for?

MARTIN. Would you believe it? My car's been taken off, on the back of a lorry. It's gone. I though I had forty minutes, but they cheated. They've got more than one lorry.

CONSTANCE. Well, if you want to use our 'phone you can. Daphne give him 10p.

MARTIN. No, no. I don't want—good heavens, Mrs. Red Hat. Hello.

MRS. FOSTER-BULLER. Have we met?

MARTIN. Yes. You remember me, don't you? In the Hall. Seat of the pants. Like Henry's?

(MARTIN turns and exhibits the seat of his pants.)

MRS. FOSTER-BULLER. Oh!! The trousers. It's Henry all over again. Do forgive me.

(MRS. FOSTER-BULLER is overcome.)

MARTIN. Oh, sorry. Was it something I—

MRS. FOSTER-BULLER. I must look a terrible sight.

DAPHNE. *(To CONSTANCE.)* Shall I put her in the spare room?

CONSTANCE. You'd better.

(DAPHNE supports MRS. FOSTER-BULLER out through the door to CONSTANCE's flat.)

CONSTANCE. Mr. Whittaker, I'm sorry to hear about your car but this has not been a very good day so far, so will you please leave?

MARTIN. I'm here on business.

CONSTANCE. You've completed your business. The computer's working. Now go away, please.

MARTIN. My money's as good as the next man's isn't it?

CONSTANCE. What money?

MARTIN. For the Course, or whatever it is you call it.

CONSTANCE. Course?

MARTIN. In hitching up.

CONSTANCE. No don't call it "hitching up" and it is not a Course. We're not offering further education.

MARTIN. I should think meeting Mrs. Foster-Buller would be a bit of an education.

CONSTANCE. So I understand that you're wanting to enroll with the Beaumont Bureau?

MARTIN. That is correct.

CONSTANCE. If I were you I would go home and consider it very carefully, for a few days. And then decide against it.

MARTIN. Just a minute, are you turning down business? I've got the money—how much is it?

CONSTANCE. Four hundred pounds.

MARTIN. Do you take checks?

CONSTANCE. I don't want your money Mr. Whittaker.

MARTIN. What's wrong with it?

CONSTANCE. Nothing, but I have an instinct for these things, and you are, I suspect, unmarriageable.

MARTIN. What?!!

CONSTANCE. Don't take it personally.

MARTIN. How d'you expect me to take it?

CONSTANCE. The Beaumont Bureau doesn't take people onto its books which it considers to be matrimonial non-starters.

MARTIN. Non-starters?

CONSTANCE. Lester Piggot wouldn't climb onto a three-legged horse.

MARTIN. Oh, is he on your books?

CONSTANCE. No.

MARTIN. Well, there aren't many three-legged horses around are there? I wouldn't have thought—

CONSTANCE. I am trying to make a point. I have nothing against you personally but you're not the sort we want.

MARTIN. I call that discrimination.

CONSTANCE. Possibly.

MARTIN. And prejudice.

CONSTANCE. Oh definitely.

MARTIN. How can you justify that?

CONSTANCE. I don't have to. I run my own business.

MARTIN. You know nothing about me. You've only just met me, and that was on a professional basis. You don't know what I'm like socially.

CONSTANCE. How old are you—forty-five?

MARTIN. Yes.

CONSTANCE. Would I be right in assuming you have never been married?

MARTIN. Yes.

CONSTANCE. Lived at home with Mother, not interested in forming relationships, with the opposite sex, until now that is ...

MARTIN. Yes.

CONSTANCE. At a guess, you were once a teacher?

MARTIN. Physics lecturer.

CONSTANCE. A man whose main interests in life are machines, equations, facts and figures.

MARTIN. And chess.

CONSTANCE. A man not interested in other people and certainly not interested in their emotions and feelings.

MARTIN. You wouldn't say that if you played chess. I have the most wonderful games with all sorts of interesting people. All night long, all over the world.

CONSTANCE. You mean in your dreams?

MARTIN. No, no. I'm a Radio Ham.

CONSTANCE. Not much fun being married to someone who's at work all day, and got earphones on all night.

MARTIN. She could have a pair of her own, she could listen in—

CONSTANCE. What a lot you have to learn Mr. Whittaker.

MARTIN. I'm willing. After all, I learnt to dance in three weeks.

CONSTANCE. You're a dancer. I'm surprised.

MARTIN. Oh yes. As soon as I get my boots and my bells on I'm a new man.

CONSTANCE. Morris Dancing?

MARTIN. I'm the one with; the bladder on a stick. I hit everybody over the head with it. It's a wonderful way of meeting people.

CONSTANCE. Yes—well—this rather confirms my suspicions. You're perfectly happy as you are, and totally unsuited to marriage.

MARTIN. Yes, but I'll take the Course and learn.

CONSTANCE. There is no Course, Mr. Whittaker.

MARTIN. How d'you get a Diploma then?

CONSTANCE. There are no Diplomas.

MARTIN. There could be, you could call it a Dip. Wed.

CONSTANCE. You could what?

MARTIN. Well if you can have a Dip. Ed. I don't see why you shouldn't have a Dip. Wed. I mean you can't expect me to know it all before I start. But if I go out with a different one each night for a week, then I'll learn a little bit from this one, a little but from that one, and then after six months I'll be ready for the real thing.

CONSTANCE. The ladies on my books Mr. Whittaker, are interested in marriage, not in providing you with a grounding in biology.

(DAPHNE enters, shutting the door behind her.)

DAPHNE. They're comforting one another. Are you still here Mr. Whittaker?

CONSTANCE. You won't believe this Daphne, but Mr. Whittaker wants to sign on with the Beaumont.

DAPHNE. Oh, bully for him.

CONSTANCE. What do you mean?

MARTIN. There you are, you see. Miss Pardoe sees nothing wrong.

CONSTANCE. *(Interrupting—to DAPHNE.)* He's unmarriageable. It'd be a complete waste of our time and money.

DAPHNE. *(Fetching an application form.)* We wouldn't be wasting our time, it would be paid for. Also, look how wrong you were about Captain Sparks.

CONSTANCE. Captain Sparks looked odd but wasn't odd. This one looks odd and *is* odd.

DAPHNE. It depends on what you mean by odd.

CONSTANCE. Well—'odd' is what I mean. O—double D—Odd.

MARTIN. Excuse me a moment. I take it we're talking about me?

CONSTANCE. I'm so sorry, yes.

MARTIN. Because my feeling is I'm no odder than most of the people on the computer. And certainly no odder than Mrs. Red Hat.

CONSTANCE. There's nothing odd about Mrs. Foster-Buller.

DAPHNE. Except her name. *(Handing form to MARTIN.)* Would you like to fill in your details?

MARTIN. Certainly. *(To CONSTANCE.)* Someone with a spark of interest.

DAPHNE. You sit there. And do ask if there's anything that puzzles you.

MARTIN. Thank you. Very kind. Nice to see somebody here knows how to run a business.

DAPHNE. We can't turn away work these days, can we?

(MARTIN sits and pores over the form.)

CONSTANCE. If you could get your head out of the financial trough, Daphne, we have got two ladies, who are Clients, in there. *(She points to her room.)* We never let female Clients bump into male Clients or vice versa.

DAPHNE. Mr. Whittaker and Mrs. Foster-Buller have already encountered one another.

CONSTANCE. But not Miss Pinder. The rules are quite clear.

DAPHNE. Do you mind if I put this screen round you—Mr. Whittaker?

MARTIN. It's not draughty, is it?

DAPHNE. It's in case Clients come in.

MARTIN. *(Not understanding.)* Oh, right.

(DAPHNE screens him from vision.)

CONSTANCE. *(Eyeing the screen.)* You know, I don't dislike that screen. Doesn't quite match the curtains.

DAPHNE. Makes them look shabby.

CONSTANCE. They're practically new.

DAPHNE. If you call twenty years old practically new.

CONSTANCE. Nothing like twenty years.

DAPHNE. It was when the Collisons got married. You had some spare fabric left over. And she made cushion covers.

CONSTANCE. Can't have been the Collisons. She couldn't boil an egg—never mind sew. What that poor man saw in that woman I'll never know.

DAPHNE. Some men like helpless women.

CONSTANCE. No woman likes a helpless man.

(MARTIN appears over the top of his screen.)

MARTIN. Where it says 'religion', shall I write 'atheist?'

CONSTANCE. Couldn't you just write—None.

MARTIN. I'm the wrong sex, aren't I? Oh, *none—I* see.

(MARTIN disappears from view.)

CONSTANCE. Atheist. I should have known. They're awfully difficult to move—atheists. It's such a depressing looking word, atheist. Like (Stafford Crippin.)

DAPHNE. If he's going to be looking for an atheist, we've only got Mrs. Rabinowitz and Miss O'Malley.

CONSTANCE. Rabinowitz and O'Malley. I though you had to be C of E to be an atheist.

(Enter MRS. FOSTER-BULLER from the door into CONSTANCE's flat.)

DAPHNE. How is Miss Pinder?

MRS. FOSTER-BULLER. She is rallying.

CONSTANCE. That's good of you.

MRS. FOSTER-BULLER. Oh, as Henry's wife I had to do rather a lot of comforting. I'm good at comforting. You develop a knack for comforting. That and Nativity Plays.

CONSTANCE. *(Interrupting.)* Don't you feel, that maybe you are likely to discourage a future pairing by continually mentioning—by harping, on Henry?

MRS. FOSTER-BULLER. Harping?

DAPHNE. Excellent man, though he was.

MRS. FOSTER-BULLER. Well he *was.*

CONSTANCE. But you can't go on saying it.

MRS. FOSTER-BULLER. I suppose you're right. Let me have another swing at that Thurston man.

CONSTANCE. No, it's too late with him. Daphne's going to re-program you on the computer. There are at least 3 new possibilities.

MRS. FOSTER-BULLER. I'm game.

DAPHNE. How do you feel about the Orkneys?

MRS. FOSTER-BULLER. Very strongly.

DAPHNE. In what way?

MRS. FOSTER-BULLER. They're Scottish aren't they? Nothing against the Scots but can't stand them.

CONSTANCE. There goes Major MacTavish.

(MARTIN rises above his screen.)

MARTIN, ALCOHOL.

CONSTANCE. What?

MARTIN. Where it says 'Alcohol', do you want the brand or the amount?

CONSTANCE. Are you teetotal?

MARTIN. No.

CONSTANCE. Then write 'Yes.' ...

(MARTIN looks puzzled and then sinks from view.)

MRS. FOSTER-BULLER. How long has that man been here? Who *is* he?

CONSTANCE. He's our computer engineer!

MRS. FOSTER-BULLER. You see, there's no doubt about the sort of man I want to get my teeth into. It's more the Home Counties type.

CONSTANCE. It's a rather restricted area, isn't it?

MRS. FOSTER-BULLER. All right, call it Network South-east. Henry was a Kentish man.

CONSTANCE. Stop mentioning Henry!

MRS. FOSTER-BULLER. Sorry.

MARTIN. *(Pops up.)* This bit at the end where it says—
"Remarks—"

CONSTANCE. Please Mr. Whittaker, will you just fill it in and stop bobbing up and down.

MARTIN. Why am I behind this screen?

CONSTANCE. Please stay out of sight.

MARTIN. Ah, you want me out of my things for a medical, yes?!

CONSTANCE. No!

DAPHNE. "Remarks" is where you write down the sort of person you're looking for.

MARTIN. Ah, well nothing with three legs for a start.

(MARTIN ducks down again.)

MRS. FOSTER-BULLER. Just a minute, he's not just a computer engineer, he's filling in a form.

CONSTANCE. I can assure you I haven't accepted him yet, he may prove to be unsuitable.

MRS. FOSTER-BULLER. He seems quite personable, and speaks the Queen's English, enough these days, heaven knows.

DAPHNE. *(Lowering her voice.)* Very personable. Five foot ten'ish, slim build.

CONSTANCE. *(Whispers.)* But atheist.

MRS. FOSTER-BULLER. Well God isn't everything, "pace" the Archbishop of Canterbury.

(MISS PINDER enters.)

CONSTANCE. How are you feeling now dear?

MISS PINDER. A little better.

CONSTANCE. Good. Go straight home and rest.

DAPHNE. Shall I call you a cab?

MISS PINDER. I don't want a cab, I want my money back.

CONSTANCE. Money back?

MISS PINDER. It's never going to work, I should never have joined in the first place.

CONSTANCE. That's defeatism. Just because your initial encounters haven't jelled.

MISS PINDER. I've been turned down you mean.

CONSTANCE. Just because you've been turned down as you choose to call it, on one or two occasions—

MISS PINDER. Eleven.

CONSTANCE. All right, eleven, it doesn't mean that twelve isn't your lucky number.

DAPHNE. Counting last night it *is* twelve.

CONSTANCE. Daphne must you. Sit down Caroline. Somewhere there's a man for you—don't lose sight of that.

MISS PINDER. I don't want to go through any more agony or embarrassment. I don't want a husband.

CONSTANCE. Yes you do. Marriage is a fine and honorable estate. You were born for it and don't let anyone tell you otherwise.

MISS PINDER. You're not married.

DAPHNE. Caroline, you're becoming personal.

MISS PINDER. And you're not either. It's not logical to pay money to people who aren't married.

CONSTANCE. I'm not married, because I choose not to be.

MISS PINDER. Well, I choose not to be, so can I have my money back?

CONSTANCE. No you may not.

MISS PINDER. Why not?

DAPHNE. We have no machinery for returning money.

MISS PINDER. I could take you to court under the Trades Descriptions Act. This shouldn't be called a Marriage Bureau. You haven't married *me*.

CONSTANCE. We're trying!

MISS PINDER. I know somebody at the BBC who works

on Esther Rantzen's show.
    CONSTANCE. Oh for heaven's sake, take your money.

(CONSTANCE crosses to her desk and angrily writes a check.)

    MRS. FOSTER-BULLER. Caroline, I hope you don't come
to regret this.
    MISS PINDER. I won't.
    MRS. FOSTER-BULLER. You may still be under the in-
fluence of Babycham.
    MISS PINDER. Last night was the worst night of my life.
    MRS. FOSTER-BULLER. It's darkest before the dawn.
Don't give up!
    DAPHNE. Why don't we see what the computer says?
    MISS PINDER. A computer won't help. How can a com-
puter help?
    DAPHNE. When I turn it on, the screen is all green, and
there are these little squares, and so I take mouse in my
right hand—
    MRS. FOSTER-BULLER. Oh please, the girl doesn't need
computers, she needs advice, comforting, something we all
know about, not wretched computers, which of us knows anything about computers?

(MARTIN's hand goes up behind the screen.)

    MISS PINDER. *(Screams.)* Ahh! What's that?
    CONSTANCE. What's what?
    MISS PINDER. A hand. It's a man's hand.

(MARTIN's head now appears.)

    CONSTANCE. Mr. Whittaker, you promised to stay out of
sight and fill up your form.
    MARTIN. But when people talk about computers as though
they were something completely mysterious and wildly

complicated I have to speak up. They are terribly simple. They're as simple as 1,2,3. Simpler in fact. It's 0,1,2. Now for a start d'you know what 'data' are? No? Well data are information which has been encoded as Nought or One or Two—any questions so far?

MRS. FOSTER-BULLER. Yes, are you busy tonight?

MARTIN. Yes, I am. So we have data and—

MISS PINDER. What about tomorrow night?

CONSTANCE. Ladies please, this is the Beaumont Bureau, not the lobby of the Regent Palace Hotel. I haven't even seen Mr. Whittaker's particulars yet. We know nothing about his education, income, prospects, background.

MARTIN. *(Proferring the form.)* There you are, it's all there.

DAPHNE. *(Taking it.)* I'll put it into the computer.

CONSTANCE. I want to see it first, Daphne.

MRS. FOSTER-BULLER. Do you like classical music? I've go tickets for the Albert Hall on Saturday.

MARTIN. Yes—why not?

MRS. FOSTER-BULLER. Door 10.

MISS PINDER. D'you object to films with sub-titles?

MARTIN. No.

MISS PINDER. There's something I'm dying to see at the Curzon.

MARTIN. Any night.

MRS. FOSTER-BULLER. But Saturday.

MARTIN. But Saturday. *(MARTIN with a lady on each side makes for the door.)* Now what are you two ladies doing? Anybody fancy an early lunch?

MRS. FOSTER-BULLER. I have to get my train to Reading before four-thirty.

MARTIN There are one or two French Restaurants near Paddington.

MRS. FOSTER-BULLER. Are you coming Caroline, or are you still feeling a little queasy?

MISS PINDER. No, I'm as fit as a flea, I could eat a horse.

MARTIN. And a filly mignon for the young lady.

*(MARTIN laughs and MISS PINDER laughs as well as the
three exit. CONSTANCE tears up the check and tosses the
pieces into the air.)*
(Curtain.)

Scene 2.

(The same. The next day.
*The curtains are closed and just a chink of sunlight warms the
room. It is 9:30 a.m. The door bell rings. Nothing happens.
It rings again. And again. The door L. opens and
CONSTANCE enters in dressing gown/housecoat. Her toi-
lette has been interrupted. She crosses to main door.)*

CONSTANCE. Who is it?

MARTIN. *(Off.)* Me.

CONSTANCE. I hate people who say 'me'. Who is it?

MARTIN. *(Off.)* Martin Whittaker.

CONSTANCE. I'm not too keen on people called Martin
Whittaker either. Come back at ten o'clock.

MARTIN. *(Off.)* I can't. I need a consultation now.

CONSTANCE. I'm not dressed.

MARTIN. *(Off.)* Oh—sorry.

CONSTANCE. *(To herself.)* Oh damn. *(She opens the door.)*
Come in.

MARTIN. *(Enters.)* I thought you said you weren't dressed.

CONSTANCE. I'm not.

(CONSTANCE opens the curtains and light streams in.)

MARTIN. You're a bit behind hand this morning. Alarm
not working?

CONSTANCE. We had a little party last night. A wedding
anniversary. The Collisons. I introduced them to one another
twenty years ago.

MARTIN. Well I take my hat off to him.

CONSTANCE. *Them*, you mean.

MARTIN. No, him. Twenty years. I've only been at it for twenty-four hours and I've come to the conclusion that women are totally different from men. Anyway, I've come to give you my report.

CONSTANCE. Well, I'd rather have this conversation after I've dressed if that's all right with you.

MARTIN. *(Looks at his watch.)* How long are you going to be? I'm a bit pushed.

CONSTANCE. We can talk while I'm dressing.

MARTIN. Right

(She goes towards her apartment. MARTIN follows her. She stops.)

CONSTANCE. No, you stay in here.

MARTIN. Oh, got you. *(CONSTANCE exits. MARTIN stays.)* Have you been in touch with Mrs. Foster-Buller or Miss Pinder?

CONSTANCE. *(Off.)* Hardly, I've only just got out of bed.

MARTIN. And they haven't been in touch with you?

CONSTANCE. *(Off.)* No.

MARTIN. Well, they were quite good company, especially for each other. They hardly drew a breath. There was quite a reasonable exchange of ideas when we were discussing the menu, but, once they got stuck into the Chardonnay I found it very difficult to interest them in normal conversation. I thought I'd keep it all simple, basic thermo dynamics, theory of relativity, but I could sense a sort of indifference. Odd really.

CONSTANCE. *(Off.)* They're not the topics I would've chosen to break the ice.

MARTIN. Oh, aren't they? Well in that case you better give me a few headings of stuff I can talk about when I take them out separately.

CONSTANCE. *(Off.)* This isn't a training school Mr. Whittaker.

MARTIN. Well it should be. I paid you four hundred pounds. Now that should include something apart from the odd name and telephone number. *(DAPHNE enters through the main door. MARTIN isn't aware of her presence and carries on talking with a raised voice.)* Give me a few pointers. If I'd never met you before, how would I get the ball rolling with you?

DAPHNE. You could lower your voice for a start.

MARTIN. *(Turns.)* Oh sorry. I wasn't talking to you.

CONSTANCE. *(Off.)* Don't mumble! Speak up!!

MARTIN. Just what it was like at lunch yesterday. Two women with two totally different sets of reactions. Except on the Theory of Relativity. Neither understood that.

CONSTANCE. *(Off.)* What?

MARTIN. It's all right, I'm talking to Miss Pardoe.

CONSTANCE. *(Miffed.)* Oh.

MARTIN. *(Helping her off with her coat.)* Hear you had a bit of a bun fight last night.

DAPHNE. I'd hardly call it that, a discreet celebration perhaps. The Collisons and us.

MARTIN. Only four? Don't they have any family or friends?

DAPHNE. Yes, but they never told anybody how they'd been brought together.

MARTIN. Why ever not?

DAPHNE. Some people, even now, prefer not to mention the role of the Bureau.

MARTIN. Really? Well I've broadcast it to the world.

DAPHNE. Pardon?

MARTIN. Last night, on my radio. Neville in Kuala Lumpur. Bjorn in Spitzbergen. And Teddy in Bulawayo. They'll all pass it on. Might bring you in a bit of business, you never know.

DAPHNE. Thank you.

MARTIN. Well I'd never heard of you had I? You could "discreet" yourself out of business. Do you advertise at all?

CONSTANCE. *(Entering.)* Only in "Good Housekeeping."

MARTIN. Can't bring in many men.

CONSTANCE. Sufficient.

MARTIN. How about "Exchange & Mart."

CONSTANCE. I'm surprised that someone who is a trained observer, like yourself, has failed to notice that we operate above a certain er—social plimsoll line.

MARTIN. *(Lost.)* Sorry?

DAPHNE. Her aunt used to insist on a public school background and a portfolio of investments.

MARTIN. What's the qualification nowadays?

CONSTANCE. A nice speaking voice.

MARTIN. Oh good. Because I haven't got a portfolio. I've got a wallet but even that's a bit thin. So I'd rather not go out twice if I can hit the nail on the head the first time. Which would you suggest, Foster-Buller or Miss Pinder?

CONSTANCE. We don't give tips.

MARTIN. I've yet to see what you do do. I've paid four hundred pounds plus lunch for three yesterday, and heaven knows how many dinners to come, and what have you done?

DAPHNE. We've processed you. All your answers are in here.

CONSTANCE. When we've analyzed you thoroughly we may find there are half a dozen possible partners for you.

MARTIN. That'll only make things more difficult. I'm perfectly happy with the two I've got. You just tell me which one you'd recommend and I'll abide by your decision.

CONSTANCE. My dear man, it's not our decision, it's yours.

MARTIN. But there's not much to choose between them. They are alike as two pins.

DAPHNE. As like as—one is 42 and extremely forthright, the other 29 and a bundle of nerves.

MARTIN. Well they both dress alike.

CONSTANCE. They dress quite differently.

MARTIN. They both wear skirts.

CONSTANCE. What?

DAPHNE. Skirts?

MARTIN. And lipstick.

CONSTANCE. Apart from skirts and lipstick they've got very little in common.

MARTIN. Oh yes they have. They're both terribly pally with some woman called Laura something.

DAPHNE. Laura?

MARTIN. Ashley! Laura Ashley. Always round at her place by the sound of it.

DAPHNE. I suppose innocence can be refreshing.

CONSTANCE. In his case it's quite frightening. *(To MARTIN.)* I don't remember when I last refunded someone's four hundred pounds, without their asking.

DAPHNE. You never have.

CONSTANCE. But I'm going to do it now. It was a mistake, I apologize. I'm entirely to blame. As soon as I can find your check, I'll give it straight back to you.

MARTIN. Steady on.

CONSTANCE. Call it a day.

MARTIN. No hang on, listen, I came here yesterday in good faith.

CONSTANCE. You came to make our computer work.

MARTIN. And by the time I'd done that, I was so impressed by your vocation here that I realized that I'd been under-achieving.

CONSTANCE. I can't think why. You've set yourself up as a computer consultant, or programmer, or whatever you call it, and you're obviously very competent.

MARTIN. I wasn't talking about work. I mean in life as a whole. A much wider sphere—living with a woman.

CONSTANCE. If that is what you have in mind, Mr. Whittaker, the sooner you take your check back the better.

MARTIN. Sorry?

DAPHNE. I imagine he means living as man and wife.

MARTIN. Well naturally, it's the ultimate in a binary system, isn't it?

CONSTANCE. I hadn't considered it in quite those terms.

MARTIN. Most people seem to end up getting married, and generally it's a pretty hit and miss affair.

CONSTANCE. Not with our Clients.

MARTIN. Precisely my point, your scheme is beautifully scientific. The random element of chance has been removed. Unless of course you've been tapped into by a 'hacker.'

CONSTANCE. I beg your pardon?

MARTIN. You haven't had a sudden speight of divorces have you?

CONSTANCE. Certainly not.

DAPHNE. We haven't had the computer that long.

MARTIN. Don't worry. I'll pop in and check it over whenever I'm passing.

CONSTANCE. Please don't give yourself the trouble.

MARTIN. It's no trouble and there'll be no charge.

DAPHNE. That's very generous of you.

CONSTANCE. But quite unnecessary. Now I really think you ought to go. Miss Pardoe and I have a busy morning ahead.

MARTIN. Indeed you have. I'm on the horns of a dilemma with these two ladies.

DAPHNE. Miss Beaumont has already solved that problem for you. We simply widen the field.

MARTIN. Pointless. If you have a two-horse race you have even chances of picking a winner. But once you have a dozen or more to choose from you might as well close your eyes and stick a pin in.

CONSTANCE. Mr. Whittaker, would you just sit down for a minute.

MARTIN. *(Looks at his watch.)* I haven't got unlimited time—

CONSTANCE. Sit down!

MARTIN. Right.

(MARTIN does so.)

CONSTANCE. The Beaumont Bureau supplies a service

to ladies and gentlemen who, after very careful consideration, have decided to embark on matrimony for companionship, for mutual interests and for love. I can say without hesitation that companionship with Mrs. Foster-Buller would be doubtful, mutual interests unlikely. She doesn't play chess, doesn't own a shortwave transmitter and is still hopelessly committed to her first husband. As for poor Miss Pinder, she's of a highly nervous disposition and will need the most sensitive handling if she's not to wither on the vine. There may well be a man somewhere who can bring her safely to the altar, but that man is definitely not you.

MARTIN. Ah, but—

CONSTANCE. I will go further. There is not one lady on our books, who could feel at ease in your company. Nothing personal you understand.

MARTIN. Sounds pretty personal.

CONSTANCE. I'm speaking from a professional point of view. I daresay you have some admirable qualities, you were probably an ideal son. But your work is your entire life. Nothing wrong in that. Miss Pardoe and I fall into that category. We're totally fulfilled aren't we?

DAPHNE. Yes.

CONSTANCE. And that's how we shall remain. And the same goes for you, Mr. Whittaker. You're a loner. Face up to it. Accept it. Enjoy it.

MARTIN. But I can't. Don't you see that? I can't any more. You've opened up new vistas for me. It's high time I burnt my boats.

CONSTANCE. But not here please.

MARTIN. I'll be honest with you, in the past I've had an occasional friendship with the opposite sex but I never knew how to tackle the situation. It was embarrassing because I never seemed to find a topic of conversation that lead anywhere.

CONSTANCE. The binary system does have its limitations.

MARTIN. You'd be surprised. Sometimes they seemed more interested in that than in me. But the point is when you meet through a marriage bureau you know *why* you've met, you know exactly what's on each other's mind, and there's no need for any of that awkward foreplay.

DAPHNE. Awkward what?

MARTIN. Er—do I mean foreplay?

CONSTANCE. God knows what you mean.

MARTIN. Well, which is it to be—Foster-Buller or Pinder?

CONSTANCE. Neither.

DAPHNE. I don't think we should be Judge and Jury Constance, and neither of the ladies has voiced any complaints.

MARTIN. You see!

CONSTANCE. You may not believe this Mr. Whittaker, but I'm rapidly coming to the conclusion that Miss Pinder and Mrs. Foster-Buller would survive the ordeal much better than you. Compared with you they're seasoned campaigners. You're so unworldly it's ridiculous, and as far as I can tell, you lack intelligence—

DAPHNE. He plays mental chess for heavens sake.

CONSTANCE. I said 'intelligence' not 'intellect.' Anyone who can park their car on the exact spot from which the Police have towed one away should be in a Home. You exist in a little world of your own. And a very nice one, too, I'm sure. But if you were ever to try to leave it, and join the rest of us, I fear for you I really do.

MARTIN. My god, you're brilliant. I'd no idea I had all these problems. But you're right, you're absolutely right. You ought to be up there with Jung and Freud. Take me on, I beg you, take me on!

CONSTANCE. Look—!!

MARTIN. Please.

CONSTANCE. Oh very well. Daphne, run him through the computer.

MARTIN. Sod the computer. I've already made my choice.

DAPHNE. Who?

MARTIN. Miss Beaumont.

CONSTANCE. Oh God.

END OF ACT I

ACT II

Scene 1

(The same. Three weeks later.
DAPHNE is working on the computer. CONSTANCE is read-
ing a letter. There are now vases with flowers everywhere.)

CONSTANCE. *(After a pause.)* Daphne, d'you remember
Isabel Smith?

DAPHNE. Thirty-three, music lover, hang-gliding, and
buck teeth.

CONSTANCE. Yes, well she hasn't got the buck teeth any
more.

DAPHNE. Oh how awful, what happened?

CONSTANCE. She ran into low cloud over Dunstable ap-
parently.

DAPHNE. Well every low cloud has a silver lining.

CONSTANCE. 'Specially for the orthodontist.

DAPHNE. Poor Miss Smith.

(CONSTANCE's phone rings.)

CONSTANCE. *(Goes for the phone and then stops her-*
self.) Daphne, 'phone.

DAPHNE. Can't you take it?

49

CONSTANCE. No I can't. It could be him again. God's gift to Interflora.

DAPHNE. *(Picks up the receiver.)* Hello, Beaumont bureau ... oh yes, Mr. Thurston, hold on a moment. *(To CONSTANCE.)* It's only Mr. Thurston.

(DAPHNE gives CONSTANCE the receiver and returns to her desk.)

CONSTANCE. Good morning Mr. Thurston. How are things in the garden? Still what? ... still v. busy, well you would be, it's that time of the year ... no, I only have a window box. 'V' small ... you're interested in Miss Pinder? Well, we hoped you would be. We've always felt there was someone special for Miss Pinder. May I suggest ... Pardon? ... What? ... Oh, yes, right. *(She replaces the receiver.)* The man's just arrived with the manure.

DAPHNE. I wonder if you were right to send Miss Pinder's details to Mr. Thurston.

CONSTANCE. Obviously I was. He's interested. Didn't you hear?

DAPHNE. She's a bit fragile for him, isn't she?

CONSTANCE. I expect he's very good with tender plants.

DAPHNE. At the moment she's totally obsessed with Martin Whittaker.

(The door bell rings.)

CONSTANCE. You answer it. That'll be him.

(CONSTANCE nips into the doorway of her apartment.)

DAPHNE. It can't always be him. You'll give yourself an ulcer—

CONSTANCE. Tell him I'm out, tell him I'm not coming back.

DAPHNE. Why don't I just say you died in your sleep?
CONSTANCE. Answer the damn door.

(DAPHNE opens the door to MRS. FOSTER-BULLER.)

DAPHNE. Good morning Mrs. Foster-Buller, how are you?
MRS. FOSTER-BULLER. *(Moving in.)* Furious!
CONSTANCE. What's happened?
MRS. FOSTER-BULLER. They're putting the fares up again.
CONSTANCE. Are they? I didn't know that.
MRS. FOSTER-BULLER. 'Course you didn't. It doesn't affect you. You and Miss Pardoe don't know you're born. Living in London and walking to work.
DAPHNE. You could live in London.
MRS. FOSTER-BULLER. 'Couldn't afford it. The only way I'll live in London is to marry into it. Now why have I not heard from Mr. Whittaker?
CONSTANCE. I've really no idea.
MRS. FOSTER-BULLER. I went to lunch with him, or rather we had lunch with him. I expect some kind of response. He's not gone off with that chip of a Pinder girl, has he?
DAPHNE. No.
MRS. FOSTER-BULLER. Then who has he gone off with?
CONSTANCE. No one.
MRS. FOSTER-BULLER. Who's he keen on? Who's he after?
CONSTANCE. It's not for us to say, is it Daphne?
DAPHNE. Don't drag me in. Mr. Whittaker's latest fancy is your problem.
MRS. FOSTER-BULLER. Ah, I thought as much. There is someone. You've passed his name to someone else. I've been gazumped.
CONSTANCE. Nothing of the kind.
MRS. FOSTER-BULLER. I'm right, aren't I Miss Pardoe?
DAPHNE. Well—

MRS. FOSTER-BULLER. What's her name?
DAPHNE. *(Sweetly.)* Why don't I make some coffee?
CONSTANCE. We've just had coffee.
DAPHNE. Well we'll have another one.

(DAPHNE exits.)

MRS. FOSTER-BULLER. I never would've imagined I could be treated in such a way by the Beaumont Bureau.
CONSTANCE. These things happen.
MRS. FOSTER-BULLER. Looking for a husband is bad enough without finding you're in the hands of a dishonest agent.
CONSTANCE. You will withdraw that remark.
MRS. FOSTER-BULLER. Only if you tell me the name of Mr. Whittaker's new woman.

(MARTIN enters through the center door, with a bunch of flowers.)

MARTIN. *(Seeing MRS. FOSTER-BULLER, cheerfully.)* My goodness me, Mrs. Foster-Buller—right? *(He approaches MRS. FOSTER-BULLER. She is mesmerized by the flowers.)* We haven't met for—how long is it?—Ten days?—Two weeks?

MRS. FOSTER-BULLER. Three weeks. What pretty flowers.

MARTIN. I did rather enjoy that luncheon. I kept thinking should I give you a ring, or drop you a note to say so, but one's never too sure of the social niceties, so I didn't.

CONSTANCE. Mr. Whittaker, I'm rather busy. Some other time perhaps—

MARTIN. Oh, well—

CONSTANCE. Off you go—

MRS. FOSTER-BULLER. Don't hound the poor man. He's come bearing gifts.

MARTIN. Gifts?

MRS. FOSTER-BULLER. Flowers. I love flowers. Are you pleased to see me?

MARTIN. Oh, always pleased to see you—Mrs. Foster-Buller.

MRS. FOSTER-BULLER. I'm sure you say the same thing to Miss Pinder.

MARTIN. Miss Pinder?

CONSTANCE. He says it to all the ladies he gives flowers to. *(To MARTIN.)* Why don't you give them to Mrs. Foster-Buller?

MARTIN. I didn't buy them for Mrs. Foster-Buller.

CONSTANCE. A detail.

MARTIN. I bought them for you.

(MARTIN gives CONSTANCE the flowers.)

MRS. FOSTER-BULLER. For *her*? For Miss Beaumont?

MARTIN. One bunch a day for three weeks!

CONSTANCE. My flat looks like a garden center.

MRS. FOSTER-BULLER. Your aunt must be turning in her grave. This is totally unethical conduct! I'm not sure it isn't actionable.

MARTIN. Giving flowers? Surely not.

CONSTANCE. *(To MARTIN.)* Why didn't you knock?

MRS. FOSTER-BULLER. You didn't want your lover to burst in, did you?

CONSTANCE. He's *not* my lover!

MARTIN. Not yet.

CONSTANCE. Not ever.

MRS. FOSTER-BULLER. What arrangements you come to, I couldn't care less. But you Miss Beaumont have behaved shamelessly. You have come between client and client. I shall complain.

CONSTANCE. To whom?

MRS. FOSTER-BULLER. The governing body. My solicitor. The *Ombudsman.*

CONSTANCE. Don't be ridiculous.

MRS. FOSTER-BULLER. Ridiculous? When you're suspended for malpractice, you won't think it's ridiculous. When I get exemplary damages *and* costs—which will be enormous—and all you get is your name in the papers, that'll wipe the smile off your face you Judas.

MARTIN. *(Puzzled but observant.)* She hasn't got a smile on her face.

MRS. FOSTER-BULLER. Jezebel!

(MRS. FOSTER-BULLER exits.)

MARTIN. What set her off?

CONSTANCE. You did.

MARTIN. Me?

CONSTANCE. And I did. Now—will you do me one very big favor?

MARTIN. Name it.

CONSTANCE. Take those flowers away.

MARTIN. But—

CONSTANCE. And, don't bring me any more.

MARTIN. Do you have an allergy?

CONSTANCE. Yes I have. I didn't know before, but now I've found out I'm allergic—to eager, badly-dressed, men in the computer industry.

MARTIN. Oh so am I. And I've met some, believe me.

CONSTANCE. I meant you.

MARTIN. You're allergic to *me*? We've only ever shaken hands.

CONSTANCE. That seems to be enough.

MARTIN. I'll bring you some anti-histamine next time.

CONSTANCE. I don't want a next time! There mustn't be a next time!!

(Enter DAPHNE with coffee.)

DAPHNE. Oh, good morning, Mr. Whittaker.

MARTIN. Miss Pardoe!

DAPHNE. What happened to Mrs. Foster-Buller?

CONSTANCE. She's gone to see her solicitor. She thinks I'm involved in some sort of insider trading.

DAPHNE. Well, she would, wouldn't she?

CONSTANCE. Whose side are you on?

DAPHNE. Oh flowers! What a lovely surprise. I hope you've brought a vase as well.

MARTIN. 'Afraid not.

DAPHNE. They're very pretty. Aren't they pretty Constance?

CONSTANCE. If you like flowers.

MARTIN. You don't know what affect you've had on me do you? I get up every morning with energy. Can't wait to be out and about.

CONSTANCE. There's the door, don't let me stop you.

MARTIN. It's funny because it's not as if I'm getting any sleep.

DAPHNE. Tossing and turning.

MARTIN. No, no, writing. I write you a long letter every night.

CONSTANCE. Perhaps you're getting the Postcode wrong. We've never received one.

MARTIN. They're not written to send.

CONSTANCE. No?

MARTIN. No. They're for you to read when I'm gone.

CONSTANCE. *(Relieved.)* Oh good. You are going then.

MARTIN. I don't mean now, I mean when I'm dead and you're a widow. Then you can read them.

CONSTANCE. No.

MARTIN. They'll be terribly touching. Listen, I've brought the one I did last night.

(MARTIN takes it from his pocket.)

CONSTANCE. Daphne, for heaven's sake, show him the door.

DAPHNE. *(Looks at her watch.)* We can spare a few minutes.

MARTIN. *(Reads.)* June the third. One a.m. Number twenty-two. My dear Miss Beaumont. My head is still reeling from seeing you today. Each day you seem to look lovelier, since I first saw you at the magic moment of 9.29 a.m. on the tenth of May. The day the earth stood still for me.

CONSTANCE. But not for me. Now—

MARTIN. I haven't finished. "The flowers were chosen to match your eyes by the way."

DAPHNE. Carnations?

CONSTANCE. Yesterday's flowers dear! Delphiniums.

MARTIN. "I have loved my visits to the flower shop ever since I met you. The colors are so much more colorful when you're in love. Yours etc. Martin Whittaker."

CONSTANCE. Thank you. Very nice.

DAPHNE. And you say there are twenty-one more like that at home?

MARTIN. Would you like to hear them?

CONSTANCE. No.

MARTIN. Have you got a Fax machine? I could then fax them.

CONSTANCE. No we haven't.

MARTIN. I could give you the gist.

CONSTANCE. Mr. Whittaker stop playing games.

MARTIN. It's been three weeks now and you still don't seem to realize that I'm serious. It's not a game. Look *(He takes a small jewelers ring box from his pocket. Shows it to CONSTANCE.)* Open it.

(CONSTANCE is momentarily thrown.)

DAPHNE. *(Tactfully.)* Perhaps this is a good moment to put these flowers in something. I'm sure we've got a thermos flask tucked away somewhere.

(DAPHNE exits with the flowers.)

MARTIN. Well, go on, it won't bite.
CONSTANCE. Put it away please.
MARTIN. What?
CONSTANCE. Put it away at once. *(Goes to her desk, and starts to write out a check.)* I'm not denying that to receive the occasional bunch of flowers is gratifying to a woman. I'm not denying that to receive the attentions of a man—
MARTIN. *(Interrupting.)* What are you doing? Are you writing me a letter?
CONSTANCE. No, a check. I'm doing something I have never done before. My aunt may turn in her grave but I'm giving you your money back.
MARTIN. I don't want it.
CONSTANCE. It's too late. You burst in here unannounced, unwanted, you offended Mrs. Foster-Buller and mortally embarrassed me. So now when I give you this check I want you to take it and go. And I never want to see hide nor hair of you again.

(CONSTANCE offers check to MARTIN.)

MARTIN. I refuse.
CONSTANCE. Take it.
MARTIN. I refuse to take it.
CONSTANCE. Don't argue.

(CONSTANCE starts to force it on MARTIN and he retreats.)

MARTIN. I won't take it.
CONSTANCE. You will!!

(CONSTANCE is chasing MARTIN round the room as DAPHNE enters.)

MARTIN. Get away.
CONSTANCE. Come here.
DAPHNE. Whoops! Excuse me.

(DAPHNE exits again.)

CONSTANCE. *(Stops chasing MARTIN.)* Daphne—come here. *(DAPHNE re-appears.)* Help me corner this man.

DAPHNE. Corner him? Have you had a change of heart?

CONSTANCE. You fool. I'm trying to give him back his fee and get rid of him.

MARTIN. I'm not going to take it.

DAPHNE. And you can't get rid of him. I want him.

CONSTANCE. What?

DAPHNE. There's something I don't understand in the word processor program. I want Mr. Whittaker to take me through it.

MARTIN. My pleasure.

CONSTANCE. That infernal machine.

DAPHNE. Who went out and bought it in the first place?

CONSTANCE. Oh shut up.

DAPHNE. You can't blame me.

MARTIN. Have you ever though that if you hadn't bought the Mitsoka 2000 S1 we might never have met?

CONSTANCE. I think of nothing else. How long are you going to be explaining this program thing?

MARTIN. Oh, not long—an hour or two.

CONSTANCE. In that case I'm going out.

MARTIN. How long for?

CONSTANCE. An hour or two, by which time you will have finished your business here and departed, never to return.

(CONSTANCE exits to her room.)

MARTIN. I don't seem to be making much progress with Miss Beaumont.

DAPHNE. I'm surprised you haven't given up.

MARTIN. Would you? In my shoes?

DAPHNE. Possibly.

MARTIN. Then you've never been in love.

DAPHNE. Possibly.

MARTIN. Well up until now I haven't. I thought I was of course, on several occasions but until you actually are—you don't know you are. I mean just the sight and sound of her and I'm rooted to the spot. I'm speechless, I can't breathe, there's a lump in my throat, I never seem to find the right thing to say. How am I ever going to get her to feel the same way. I've tried softening her up. I give her flowers every day. Doesn't she like flowers?

DAPHNE. In moderation.

MARTIN. It's too late for moderation. I switched on my "personal organizer" the other day and do you know how old I am?

DAPHNE. 'Course I do. It was me put all your details on the computer.

MARTIN. Oh yes, well, I've got no secrets from you have I? You know all about me, all my facts, all my foibles, but what do I know about Miss Beaumont? *(CONSTANCE comes through wearing a summer coat and carrying a handbag, she goes to the main door. MARTIN moves towards her.)* What do I know about you?

CONSTANCE. *(Opening the door.)* Bugger all.

(CONSTANCE exits.)

MARTIN. Well—she's still speaking to me. That's something. Maybe I should switch from flowers to fruit. D'you think that would do it?

DAPHNE. I've never see her eat fruit, but I like it.

MARTIN. Chocolates then?

DAPHNE. Yes, we love chocolates. She eats the soft centers and I eat the hard.

MARTIN. You'd make a good double act. That's one of my problems, you're always here. You cramp my style, you know. Like having someone looking over your shoulder when you're playing chess.

DAPHNE. I always pop out to make the coffee.

MARTIN. How long does that take? Two minutes. Barely time to get your pawns into play, never mind developing your "middle game."

DAPHNE. Or going on to mate in fourteen moves.

MARTIN. *(Somewhat shocked.)* Miss Pardoe, please, you'll make me blush. Now what's your problem with the word processing?

DAPHNE. *(Ignoring the question.)* If you want to get Miss Beaumont on her own, come here after office hours.

MARTIN. She'd never let me in. Funny you know, she took agin me from the start.

DAPHNE. Well, as I remember you did rather poke fun at the idea of a marriage bureau.

MARTIN. Yes, but then I changed my mind didn't I? I joined up and forked out four hundred pounds, but she still won't accept any of my invitations.

DAPHNE. You irritate her.

MARTIN. *(Amazed.)* Do I?

DAPHNE. Yes, profoundly. The moment you come through the door her hackles rise.

MARTIN. Oh dear. You think I'm wasting my time then?

DAPHNE. Actually no, I don't. May I tell you something?

MARTIN. If you've got any pointers I'm all ears.

DAPHNE. It's not advice, it's just a story. I've got a friend who took up with a man or rather he took up with her. He was very persistent but she really wasn't interested. In fact she found him rather irritating.

MARTIN. Why?

DAPHNE. She was set in her ways, used to being on her own. He showered her with invitations but she said 'No' most of the time. And then, one day, he knocked her for six.

MARTIN. He hit her?

DAPHNE. He told her she had beautiful eyes.

MARTIN. And did she? Has she?

DAPHNE. Not particularly.

MARTIN. He was lying then.

DAPHNE. No he meant it.

MARTIN. Oh! Because he was in love with her he saw something that other people didn't.

DAPHNE. Yes.

MARTIN. Did they get married?

DAPHNE. Not yet, but they're having a wonderful affair.

MARTIN. Do you tell this story to all your faltering Clients?

DAPHNE. No, to be perfectly frank I've never told it before—and it's such a relief to get it off my chest.

MARTIN. Why's that?

DAPHNE. Because I've been keeping it a secret.

MARTIN. Oh, your friend, she wanted it kept quiet?

DAPHNE. I haven't got a friend.

MARTIN. You mean now you've spilt the beans she'll never speak to you again? Well that's life!

DAPHNE. It's me!!

MARTIN. What is?

DAPHNE. Forget it. Let's get on with this program. *(Picks up the program book.)* I think I've got pages missing.

MARTIN. Worry not, I've got another book in the car.

(He exits. DAPHNE sighs, sits down at her desk and takes a framed photograph out of the drawer. She looks at it as MARTIN comes dashing back in.)

MARTIN. You can't fool me, it's you!!

(Curtain.)

Scene 2

(The same. That evening.

*The Stage is empty. The lights are out and the curtains are
    open. It is dusk. There is a ring at the door. After a moment
    CONSTANCE enters with a book in her hand and listens.
    She is about to return to her room as the bell goes again.
    She crosses to the door.)*

CONSTANCE. *(Looks at her watch.)* Who is it?

DAPHNE. *(Off.)* Constance, I'm sorry to disturb you at
this hour—it's me Daphne, I've left my glasses in the drawer.

CONSTANCE. *(Opens the door and walks away from it.)*
It's not like you—forgetting things.

*(MARTIN enters with a tape recorder slung round his neck
    and a triumphant smile on his face. He clicks off the re-
    corder.)*

MARTIN. 'Evening.

CONSTANCE. *(Spins round.)* What are you doing here,
where's Daphne? Where's Daphne gone?

MARTIN. Into the ether. *(Removes the recorder.)* Gone,
lost, leaving just me.

CONSTANCE. How dare you come here at this hour.

MARTIN. I'll come back later.

CONSTANCE. I don't want you here at all.

MARTIN. Your wish is my command. *(He exits.)* Or rather
it would be—*(re-enters)*, if I hadn't spent so much on a hamper.

*(He kicks the door closed behind him and moves to the desk to
    put the Hamper down.)*

CONSTANCE. Mr. Whittaker—

MARTIN. Have you eaten?

CONSTANCE. Yes.

MARTIN. Good, because this is just a snack. *(He opens the Hamper and removes the contents.)* Champagne, glasses, smoked salmon, caviar—

CONSTANCE. Just take it away, and yourself.

MARTIN. *(Ignoring her.)* And the pièce de resistance—ta-ra—an orchid! *(He takes out a cellophane packet.)* Are you any good at opening champagne bottles?

CONSTANCE. No, I'm not.

MARTIN. Then it's a bit of luck I'm here—I am.

(MARTIN starts to open bottle.)

CONSTANCE. I could ring the Police.

MARTIN Please don't. There's only two glasses. Come on, relax.

CONSTANCE. How can I relax when you burst in here unannounced.

MARTIN. But I was announced—by Daphne.

CONSTANCE. My God yes. Did Daphne record that?

MARTIN. She knows all your details, and she had another look at mine and thought perhaps we were rather well-suited.

CONSTANCE. She what?!!

MARTIN. Not Romeo and Juliet perhaps, but something more on a par with—oh I dunno—Beatrice and Benedict.

CONSTANCE. What on earth does she think she is—a marriage bureau? *(Suddenly realizes.)* Well of course she *is* a marriage bureau but she has absolutely no right to interfere with my life.

MARTIN. *(Hands her a glass of champagne.)* I said exactly the same thing to her. I said—"Daphne", I said, I said "Constance won't like to hear that you've been bandying her name around coupling it with mine. Shall we sit down?

CONSTANCE. Daphne hasn't the remotest idea of my details, she—no, I won't sit down.

MARTIN. Oh come on. What's nicer than a good belly-ache about a colleague in the office?

CONSTANCE. The woman's a snake in the grass.

MARTIN. That's right. D'you know every pub in London at lunchtime is full of people complaining about the people they work with.

CONSTANCE. I wouldn't know.

MARTIN. Oh yes. They're not arguing about politics or religion, they're agreeing. They're all agreeing about the idiot who works beside them. And here's you and I agreeing. It's exactly the same with us, except in this pub the food's a bit better.

CONSTANCE. *(She sits.)* Yes. I've trusted her for twenty years, and now what does she do?

MARTIN. She helps me put a foot in the door. A little smoked salmon?

CONSTANCE. I'm not hungry.

MARTIN. Oh. Well I'll never eat all this myself. I'll have to throw it away. Seems criminal to waste food. *(Finds waste-paper basket.)* In here do?

CONSTANCE. Oh all right. I'll have some.

MARTIN. You can always tell the people brought up during rationing.

(MARTIN offers her the plate.)

CONSTANCE. I was born after rationing. *(Takes the plate.)* Thank you.

MARTIN. *(Surprised.)* Sorry?

CONSTANCE. What?

MARTIN. You said 'thank you'.

CONSTANCE. Yes.

MARTIN. That's the first nice thing you've ever said to me.

CONSTANCE. Savor it.

MARTIN. Oh I am doing. *(Handing her a plate of salmon.)* There's plenty of lemon and black pepper. D'you want black pepper?

CONSTANCE. *(Calmly.)* Yes please.

MARTIN. Oh those phrases—yes please—

CONSTANCE. *(Takes the lemon.)* Thank you.

MARTIN. Oh—"thank you"—beautiful.

CONSTANCE. You're being facetious?

MARTIN. No I'm not. Do you know the most wonderful thing about you?

CONSTANCE. There aren't any wonderful things about me.

MARTIN. Your voice.

CONSTANCE. My voice?

MARTIN. I've fallen in love with your voice.

CONSTANCE. Don't exaggerate.

MARTIN. I'm not.

CONSTANCE. You haven't fallen in love. You're a bit—a bit silly about me, that's all.

MARTIN. You second. Your voice first.

CONSTANCE. I've never heard such rubbish.

MARTIN. No, it's true. You can fall in love with a voice. You remember "Family Favorites'?

CONSTANCE. *(Puzzled.)* 'Family Favorites'?

MARTIN. *(Sings.)* La la la. La la la.

CONSTANCE. Oh yes. Vaguely, yes.

MARTIN. Well, there was Cliff Michelmore in Germany and Jean Metcalfe in London. They'd never met. And every week he used to hear her voice introducing the records. And he fell under the spell of that voice. And on the strength of that voice, he proposed, and she accepted, and they married.

CONSTANCE. What did she think about his voice?

MARTIN. History doesn't relate. They're still married.

CONSTANCE. Perhaps we should add something about the voice to people's details.

MARTIN. I can put it in the computer.

CONSTANCE. Difficult to describe—a voice.

MARTIN. Warm, mellow, sensuous, mellifluous—

CONSTANCE. Some would be shrill, boring—

MARTIN. I was talking about *your* voice.

CONSTANCE. This isn't the first drink you've had tonight, is it?

MARTIN. It absolutely is. Was yours a happy childhood?

CONSTANCE. What?

MARTIN. Was yours a happy childhood?

CONSTANCE. Well—

(A Silence.)

MARTIN. I mean, give it a mark out of ten.

CONSTANCE. Er—

(Another long silence.)

MARTIN. There aren't going to be many of these long silences are there?

CONSTANCE. What?

MARTIN. Only I'm supposed to speak to Ted in Bulawayo at twelve o'clock.

CONSTANCE. What a strange life you do lead.

MARTIN. It looks like he might "castle king side." He's either very clever or very stupid and I'm dying to know which.

CONSTANCE. I'm surprised to know you could find the time to pop round here.

MARTIN. You didn't answer my question—marks out of ten.

CONSTANCE. Oh—I don't know.

MARTIN. Well, was it a happy childhood?

CONSTANCE. No, not particularly, it wasn't. Should it have been?

MARTIN. Well, yes, it should. Were you ill-treated?

CONSTANCE. No. More ignored. Sent away to school. Couldn't wait to grow up and get out.

MARTIN. You missed all the best bits. School. School holidays. Always something to do. Cricket or skating. Exploring—you know—messing about in boats, radio sets, fiddling about with things.

CONSTANCE. Are you talking about then, or now?

MARTIN. Both ... I suppose. Now you mention it, *(Laughs.)* wonderful thing school. Pull it on like a coat. That's why I stayed on and was a teacher. And, of course, I lived at home.

CONSTANCE. Why 'of course?'

MARTIN. My father died when I was very young so naturally my mother didn't want to be all alone, so I went to a day school.

CONSTANCE. That explains a lot. Mother's boy.

MARTIN. Yes. I was very fortunate that way.

CONSTANCE. But you've missed out on the hurly-burly of life.

MARTIN. Not really, mother was a dispatch-rider during the War.

CONSTANCE. Heavens. How do people like that settle down in peace time?

MARTIN. Wasn't easy. But then she got lucky. Got a job on the Wall of Death on Canvey Island.

CONSTANCE. Am I supposed to believe this?

MARTIN. Please yourself. I wouldn't make that up, would I?

CONSTANCE. I suppose not. Well at least your childhood must've been more interesting than mine.

MARTIN. Oh go on. You must've done things. You must've had some hobbies.

CONSTANCE. Nothing much, no time for them.

MARTIN. Why not?

CONSTANCE. Too busy trying to please teacher.

MARTIN. Coming top of the class you mean?

CONSTANCE. No, no. Polishing Miss Marchbank's bicycle. Trying to sit at Miss Hart's feet in the school photograph—

MARTIN. Did you have a scowl and pigtails?

CONSTANCE. No, I had a scowl and freckles.

MARTIN. Ah. And then you got spots.

CONSTANCE. No, I never had any spots. Did you?

MARTIN. Well, no, not really, come to think of it.

CONSTANCE. Most adolescents do.

MARTIN. I'm not sure I was ever adolescent, I mean my voice broke and I started shaving, but I don't remember being rebellious and all that.

CONSTANCE. Well, you're making up for it now.

MARTIN. Rebellious? I'm not being rebellious.

CONSTANCE. You're being bloddy-minded. I mean look at all those flowers. You've been bombarding me with bunches every day.

MARTIN. Yes I'm sorry. From now on, I'll just send you a single orchid every day, by messenger.

CONSTANCE. We'll refuse it. I shall instruct Daphne that on no account—*(She stops.)* except of course, that would be a waste of time, I can't trust her anymore. Just wait 'till I see her tomorrow. No, I'll tell her what I think of her now.

(She goes to the phone.)

MARTIN. She won't be in.

CONSTANCE. How do you know?

MARTIN. It's Thursday. She's never in on Thursdays.

CONSTANCE. Isn't she?

MARTIN. No, that's the night she stays with whatshisname.

CONSTANCE. She what?!!

MARTIN. Ah, oh,—er—er—didn't you know?

CONSTANCE. Know what?

MARTIN. Ah, no you don't. (Hastily.) There's this aunt she goes to.

CONSTANCE. What*his*name you said.

MARTIN. Look please, you mustn't ask me. I'm amazed you don't know, she hasn't told you about it. But it's up to her to tell you, not me.

CONSTANCE. She's got a man, she's suddenly got a male friend hasn't she?

MARTIN. No, not suddenly, it's been jogging along for years.

CONSTANCE. Years?

MARTIN. Well, yes.

CONSTANCE. Why has she never told me? Why has she never told me?

MARTIN. Why are you so upset? I mean you don't have to be a vestal virgin to work in a marriage bureau do you?

CONSTANCE. *(Realizing.)* I know why she hasn't told me. It's some man on the files isn't it? She's been poaching. It's not done. It's unethical.

MARTIN. Well if you work in a chocolate factory and you've got a sweet tooth you're bound to have the occasional nibble.

CONSTANCE. What's his name?

MARTIN. Oh please, don't ask me.

CONSTANCE. What's his name. Tell me or get out.

MARTIN. You mean if I tell you I can stay?? Anthony Wagstaff.

CONSTANCE. Wagstaff. Rings a bell. Where are those blessed cards of hers. *(CONSTANCE roots around looking for them. MARTIN casually walks over to the computer. CONSTANCE finds the box and rifles through it.)* They're all over the place—Whitelaw, Wainwright, Walker, Widmerpool—

(MARTIN taps out "Wagstaff" on the computer.)

MARTIN. Here you are. Wagstaff. Anthony. He's here all right.

CONSTANCE. *(Dashes over to look.)* Born 1940. Five feet seven. Blue eyes. Civil Servant. Rambling. Bridge. Good talk. Fee accepted, 10th March 1987. Introductions nil. My God, he's been on the books for 5 years and he's never met anyone.

MARTIN. Except Daphne, every Thursday.

CONSTANCE. How could she do it? For five years. How could she?

MARTIN. She must find him attractive.

CONSTANCE. I mean how could she deceive me? She's hi-jacked a Client.

MARTIN. Well, he's not complaining.

CONSTANCE. I've shared this office with Daphne for twenty years, and for the last five years she's been lying to me.

MARTIN. That's not strictly true. You've never said to Daphne—"What's this you're getting up to every Thursday night with Tony Wagstaff? And she's never said—"Who is Tony Wagstaff?"

CONSTANCE. Don't stand up for the woman! She connived with you in the most underhand way to make that recording of her voice and she—

MARTIN. *(Interrupting.)* Daphne was very sympathetic. She knows how I feel about you. She understands those yearning feelings.

CONSTANCE. Yes. She gets them every Thursday night.

MARTIN. Think how I feel!! I've had them every night for three weeks.

CONSTANCE. Oh, you and your feelings!

MARTIN. Look, why is it that if my feelings were directed at Miss Pinder you'd take them seriously but because they're directed at you, you don't?

CONSTANCE. Because if they were directed at Miss Pinder, that would be allowable according to the rules of the game. Directing them at me is outside the rules of the game.

MARTIN. You mean you're not allowed a snort if you're peddling the stuff?

CONSTANCE. I've no idea what you're talking about and if I did, I'm sure I'd find it very offensive.

MARTIN. Why are you outside the game?

CONSTANCE. It's just because I'm not interested.

MARTIN. I thought I wasn't interested. In fact up until I walked through this door, I wasn't.

CONSTANCE. I wish you'd never walked through that door.

MARTIN. Half of me almost agrees with you, but the other half says if I hadn't, I would never have heard that voice. And even if I never saw you again, I wouldn't forget the voice. You can't unremember things.

CONSTANCE. A voice you certainly can. Tomorrow morning I won't even know what you sound like.

MARTIN. Possibly. But you won't forget that very special thing I said.

CONSTANCE. What special thing was that?

MARTIN. I haven't said it yet. Here, have some more champagne.

CONSTANCE. I think I'm going to need it.

MARTIN. I think you are.

CONSTANCE. *(Looking at her watch.)* What about Ted in Bulawayo?

MARTIN. I'll be there in time for him. *(He switches on his tape recorder.)* Listen.

CONSTANCE. It's not more of Daphne, is it?

MARTIN. Sshh. *(We hear music—Arabella.)* It is Strauss.

CONSTANCE. You want us to waltz?

MARTIN. Not Johann. Richard. Like it?

CONSTANCE. It's—quite nice.

MARTIN. Nice? It's obvious you don't know the first thing about Strauss.

CONSTANCE. Well—it doesn't sound as good as his father's stuff.

MARTIN. It's not the same family. Forget the oom pah pah. This is Richard. This is music of the highest sensuality. The greatest music ever written for the female voice. *(We hear a soprano voice.)* When you hear that, you can imagine heaven. You get a glimpse through the gates of Paradise.

CONSTANCE. Well, I must be tone-deaf because—

MARTIN. Listen! And if you listen hard enough—then just for a moment you don't know who you are or where you are, but you know you don't want to be anywhere else. *(They listen for a time, then he snaps the tape recorder off.)* And that's how I feel about you.

(CONSTANCE sits still for a moment or two and then drains her champagne.)

CONSTANCE. Please don't do that again.

MARTIN. Do what?

CONSTANCE. Play music and say things like that. Because whatever it is you feel, I don't feel the same thing. And it makes me unhappy being left out.

MARTIN. Oh dear. I didn't come here to make you unhappy.

CONSTANCE. Miss Pinder, or Mrs. Foster-Buller might like the music—

MARTIN. Please, don't be practical! This isn't a practical problem and it doesn't have a practical answer.

CONSTANCE. I'm sorry, that's me. I'm practical. Practical enough to know that you and I aren't meant for each other. Or whatever the phrase is they use nowadays.

MARTIN. You should know the phrase, it's your line of country.

CONSTANCE. The Bureau is a business. It stays aloof. It doesn't get emotionally involved.

MARTIN. You don't have to apply that principle to your own life. You're underpowered. You're like a computer, but you haven't switched on all your circuits.

CONSTANCE. And I don't intend to, Professor. I was enjoying a quiet switched off evening with my book, until you smuggled your way in.

MARTIN. You book? What sort of books do you read?

CONSTANCE. *(Points to it.)* I was just starting it, what's

the title? It won the Booker Prize this year.

MARTIN. Oh god, don't bother with that thing. It begins dull and then tails off.

CONSTANCE. I'm enjoying it. And I certainly wouldn't go by your 'say so'. So take your picnic and your music, and your flowers—

MARTIN. Oh please, keep the orchid.

CONSTANCE. *(Getting angry.)* No! I've got quite enough flowers form you! Not one more!!

MARTIN. It would give me hope.

CONSTANCE. No. If I'd been firm enough to hand you back the flowers three weeks ago, we wouldn't have landed in this ridiculous position now!

MARTIN. I'm not in a ridiculous position—I'm in love.

CONSTANCE. Well I'm not and it is. And whatever other ruses you dream up, we're chalk and cheese and I'm not going to marry you.

MARTIN. I wasn't going to ask you to marry me. I was going to ask you out to dinner tomorrow night.

CONSTANCE. And I'm sure they're one and the same thing in your mind.

MARTIN. Well, yes, they are.

CONSTANCE. I hope you won't lay any of this at my door, Mr. Whittaker. None of this has been my doing I've made my feelings plain from the start.

MARTIN. *(Defeated.)* Yes, yes, you have.

CONSTANCE. Now, I know I've said you're not to come back to service—or whatever—this machine, but you're in business, the same as I am, so I won't stop you from earning your living.

MARTIN. No, no. Thank you all the same but I couldn't. I don't need a heartache every few days, do I?

CONSTANCE. Aren't you being over dramatic?

MARTIN. No. You'd like to think so. But no, I'm not ... so ... well ...

CONSTANCE. I'm sorry.

MARTIN. Well, it's good-bye. Since there's no hope.

CONSTANCE. Oh wait. *(She hurries off to her room. He waits full of hope. She returns.)* Pop this on the doorstep for me.

(It is an empty milk bottle—gleaming.)

MARTIN. *(Admiringly.)* Yes—that's practical.

(MARTIN exits. CONSTANCE turns off the office light. The stage is still partly lit from her apartment. She picks up her book, walks towards her door, stops, looks at the book, tosses it away irritably and exits, shutting the door.)

Scene 3

(The same. The following morning. All the flowers have been removed. CONSTANCE is hard at work, writing at her desk. The 'phone rings.)

CONSTANCE. *(Lifts the receiver.)* Beaumont Bureau—No, this is Miss Beaumont speaking—Well won't I do, Miss Pardoe isn't in yet—yes I know its gone ten, but it is Friday morning and last night was Thursday night—no, I've no idea what I mean. Now why don't you give *me* the details because Miss Pardoe may not be with the Bureau much longer—no not early retirement, the early boot—you've changed your mind. Suit yourself. *(She replaces the receiver. The 'phone rings again immediately. She answers is brusquely.)* Yes? *(Then sweetly.)* —I mean Beaumont Bureau, good morning, Miss Beaumont speaking—you saw our advertisement—yes, there's an enrollment fee of four hundred pounds—I'll send you our brochure under plain cover if you can give me your name and address—Mrs. Sigurney—S ... I ...

(DAPHNE enters.)

DAPHNE. Morning.
CONSTANCE. Ah! *(Then into 'phone.)* What?—G ... O ... U ... R ... N ... A ... Y. What? E ... Y. *(She is desperate to get at DAPHNE.)* Yes, what's the address? What Cottage? Yglass Cottage. How on earth do you spell that? Y ... G ... L ... A ... Double S ... Right, and that's where? Llandu—Oh God, give me a telephone number and I'll call you back—0 ... 6 ... 3 ... what? 0 ... 3 ... 6? Oh you mean 0 ... 8 ... 3 ... 5—*(Her patience snaps.)* We've been cut off. *(She slams down the receiver.)* I wonder you have the nerve to show your face in here.
DAPHNE. Did you let him in?
CONSTANCE. Of course I let him in, thanks to your silly trick.
DAPHNE. Oh dear. You didn't enjoy his visit.
CONSTANCE. No I did not, and why you should have helped him God knows.
DAPHNE. We're in the business of helping men to—
CONSTANCE. *(Cutting in.)* You've been lying to me.
DAPHNE. Have I?
CONSTANCE. We've shared this office for twenty years Daphne. We've shared our thoughts, our hopes, we've been chums. And now find that for the past five years you've been coming into on a Friday morning with that demure butter-wouldn't-melt-in-your-mouth look that you have every other morning. And you've just come straight from your little blue-eyed boy—Rambling Anthony Wagstaff.
DAPHNE. Oh dear. I knew it was a mistake to tell Mr. Whittaker.
CONSTANCE. You've had your hand in the till haven't you?
DAPHNE. I've never taken a penny.

CONSTANCE. I'm not talking about petty cash. Anthony Wagstaff was a Client. He'd paid his fee—he was entitled to proper treatment.

DAPHNE. Oh I think I give him proper treatment.

CONSTANCE. I mean from this Bureau. We have a queue of women who would have given their eye teeth for a meeting with Mr. Wagstaff, and you had the nerve to take him out of circulation.

DAPHNE. Constance you're exaggerating.

CONSTANCE. You're not a Client, you never registered.

DAPHNE. Of course not.

CONSTANCE. You owe me four hundred pounds.

DAPHNE. Oh, for heaven's sake.

CONSTANCE. This is a business we're running, not the Red Cross. We're desperately short of men. We've got half a dozen women for every man. I can't afford to have one stolen.

DAPHNE. Supposing when Mr. Wagstaff had come in, *you'd* fallen for him.

CONSTANCE. The point is I didn't, and the fact is I don't ever remember him.

DAPHNE. September 9th 1987. He had a green overcoat, and a hat with a little feather!

CONSTANCE. Not him!!

DAPHNE. Yes.

CONSTANCE. Him? The midget with pop-eyes.

DAPHNE. He's a nice looking man.

CONSTANCE. He's got his hair scraped right over to hide a bald patch.

DAPHNE. If he's as bad as you say then perhaps it's just as well I'd taken him off your hands.

CONSTANCE. Why did you never tell me?

DAPHNE. *(Pause.)* Well I did in the end. Telling Martin Whittaker was tantamount to telling you. I think I must've done that one purpose.

CONSTANCE. You kept it to yourself for five years.

DAPHNE. It wasn't easy.

CONSTANCE. That's why you come home now with so few holiday snaps.

DAPHNE. Do I?

CONSTANCE. You used to bore me stiff with piles of them. Now there's only three or four. You had to take out the ones with Mr. Wagstaff in.

DAPHNE. The reason I didn't tell you was because of all the years we worked here together. I've always enjoyed it— the way we talk. The way we get on, and I thought things would never be the same if you knew about Tony.

CONSTANCE. You must've been laughing behind your hands at me, letting me run on, pouring out all my private thoughts, imagining you were a single woman like myself. Silly school-girl confidences, I thought we were sharing and all the time you're—you're dashing away with the smoothing iron, with Mr. Wagstaff.

DAPHNE. Well, I have tried to suggest on occasions that I'm not totally averse to male company.

CONSTANCE. Well you didn't try hard enough. You must've thought me a perfect fool.

DAPHNE. Not at all, but I was quite right to keep it secret because look at you, you're eaten up with jealousy.

CONSTANCE. I am nothing of the kind.

DAPHNE. Then why call Tony bald—why call him a midget and pop-eyed?

CONSTANCE. That may have been a thumb-nail sketch, but perfectly valid.

DAPHNE. Just as I thought, jealousy. You obviously didn't enjoy your yesterday evening.

CONSTANCE. Most of it, I did.

DAPHNE. Really?

CONSTANCE. All of it up to the point when the Mad Hatter burst in with his tea party, thanks to you.

DAPHNE. Oh good, then he got to Fortnums in time.

CONSTANCE. I know what you hoped it would do. You hoped it would pair me off, just like you're paired off. I was supposed to walk off into that sunset with Martin Whittaker, while you walk off into that sunset *(Points.)* with whathisname Wagstaff. How far are you prepared to go for the sake of symmetry? The whole idea is preposterous.

DAPHNE. You're past it. No man would give you a second thought, and who could blame him. You're a born spinster, you're on the shelf. You're not going to inspire anyone to look up, never mind reach out.

CONSTANCE. I'm proud of it. All women have a perfect right to be spinster "On the Shelf" is a sexist idea. A woman's status shouldn't be defined by whether she's married or unmarried. For heaven's sake why are we so pre-occupied with marriage.

DAPHNE. Because this is a marriage bureau.

CONSTANCE. Oh yes.

(The phone rings on DAPHNE's desk.)

DAPHNE. *(Goes to pick it up.)* I need a coffee. If this is going to be my last day here, you can make it.

(CONSTANCE exits in high dudgeon.)

DAPHNE. Hello? Sorry to keep you waiting. Beaumont Bureau. Mr. Thurston?—And a v. good morning to you, too. You've had a 'phone conversation with Miss Pinder? That is good news—*(Disappointment.)*—Oh—I beg you to think again Mr. Thurston. You could be missing out on a gem there. She is timid. She has bouts of shyness, that's all—what young maiden doesn't?—well, as far as we know she is, yes, not speaking from experience I'd say it's the shy ones who really open out if you pay them enough attention—like what?—dahlias? Yes why not. That's right. There's no way you can do too much preparation on the bed. I mean the plot. Just keep her away from the Babycham and go for it, Thurston!—You're welcome.

(DAPHNE puts the phone down. CONSTANCE re-enters.)

CONSTANCE. And if you must know, I'm not past it.

DAPHNE. What?

CONSTANCE. I inspired him. I inspired Mr. Whittaker. *He* didn't think I was past it. He was wooing me—with champagne, and caviar and smoked salmon. *And* an orchid. Look— *(She shows it.)* Have you ever got one of these from Willy Wagstaff?

DAPHNE. Tony Wagstaff.

CONSTANCE. Tony, Willy—what's the difference?

DAPHNE. Quite a lot.

CONSTANCE. He serenaded me, Daphne.

DAPHNE. With a guitar?

CONSTANCE. With a whole orchestra. It was a tape of— what's that big musical family in Germany?

DAPHNE. Von Trapp?

CONSTANCE. No.

DAPHNE. Bach?

CONSTANCE. No—Strauss. Not the waltz one but the one who wrote for women's voices. Because it's my voice that's inspired him. He's fallen in love with my voice.

DAPHNE. Your voice?

CONSTANCE. Yes. He's eccentric of course, but harmless enough.

DAPHNE. Harmless? Well marriages have been built on less.

CONSTANCE. Except I'm not interested.

DAPHNE. Well maybe you should be. One of these days you're going to be sitting on that sofa in there—or in some Old People's Home—all alone. With not even someone to look forward to on visitor's day.

CONSTANCE. *You'll* come and visit me surely?

DAPHNE. I'm older than you are Constance. I'll have popped off in a flurry of happy activity.

CONSTANCE. You make it sound like marriage is the only answer to life.

DAPHNE. Of course it isn't. Not for nuns, anyway. But when some man comes along and says he loves you—

CONSTANCE. The point is I don't love him. He's not "Mr. Right".

DAPHNE. Mr. Right? I never thought I'd hear you use that phrase. That's what parlormaids used to say—"One day I'm hoping to meet Mr. Right".

CONSTANCE. You seem to have met yours—Mr. Wonderful Wagstaff.

DAPHNE. Tony? No. He's sort, pop-eyed and going bald but he says he loves me. There are not Mr. Rights only lots of Mr. Wrongs, some of whom are less wrong than others.

CONSTANCE. Yes, well, keep that little insight to yourself, don't spread it amongst the customers.

DAPHNE. No, they must continue the search, at four hundred pounds an introduction, or the Bureau goes bust.

CONSTANCE. The longer they search the more money we make it's true, but if it's love at first sight, I'm equally happy.

DAPHNE. I'm glad to think that Tony and I will have your blessing. We are getting married.

CONSTANCE. *(Flabbergasted.)* Married? To this Wagstaff?

DAPHNE. Well, there isn't anyone else.

CONSTANCE. He's asked you?

DAPHNE. With a little prompting.

CONSTANCE. And you've said yes?

DAPHNE. Aren't you going to congratulate me?

CONSTANCE. In a minute I expect.

DAPHNE. I'm thinking about leaving.

CONSTANCE. Leaving? No Daphne you can't. A friendship like ours isn't something to be tossed aside. We've had such a happy partnership and if a little increase in salary would help, then I'm sure I can manage it somehow. Relationships like ours are all too rare—don't throw it away.

DAPHNE. You're very kind, Constance, but no.

CONSTANCE. I'm not kind at all, I just can't work that bloody machine.

DAPHNE. I told you not to get it in the first place. Actually, it's quite easy.

CONSTANCE. *(Lets fly.)* Don't tell me it's quite easy!! I don't want to hear about it. Marriage or no marriage, just stay here and work it.

DAPHNE. You'll have to learn to use it. I shall be away on my honeymoon for a start.

CONSTANCE. What d'you want a honeymoon for? You've been having one every Thursday.

DAPHNE. A proper one.

CONSTANCE. You could take a week.

DAPHNE. No, no, at least a month.

CONSTANCE. A month?

DAPHNE. Or two.

CONSTANCE. I'm not going to spend the next twenty years being held to ransom.

DAPHNE. There's a rather ugly side to you Constance. "Held to Ransom" indeed. If that's how you see it, the simplest thing is for me to leave.

CONSTANCE. You can't leave.

DAPHNE. *(Picks up her bag.)* Once upon a time no I couldn't, because when I left I wasn't going anywhere, but now I've got somewhere to go. It is a great relief. I recommend it. Good-bye. *(She reaches the door.)* I'm giving you a month's notice.

CONSTANCE. I refuse to accept it, or even speak to you until you pull yourself together.

(She exits L. closing her door.)

DAPHNE. And a happy Christmas to you too. *(She flings open the main door and comes face to face with MARTIN.)* Martin—

MARTIN. Good morning. May I come in?

DAPHNE. Yes. Though I can't imagine why you should want to.

MARTIN. How's Miss Beaumont this morning?

DAPHNE. Unspeakable.

MARTIN. She threw me out. I expect it's remorse.

DAPHNE. I wouldn't bank on it. It's me she's got it in for.

MARTIN. What've you done?

DAPHNE. Got myself a boy friend. She's jealous. I would never have believed it of her, but she's eaten up with it.

MARTIN. Good. Then I know exactly how to tackle her and win her over.

DAPHNE. You know more than I do.

MARTIN. I shall spin her a yarn—

(CONSTANCE enters through door L. at speed.)

CONSTANCE. Daphne, I've decided to accept your— (Stops.) Mr. Whittaker.

MARTIN. Forgive the intrusion. May I have a word?

(CONSTANCE does not answer.)

DAPHNE. May he?

CONSTANCE. Is it about the computer?

MARTIN. Well, actually no.

CONSTANCE. I didn't think it would be.

MARTIN. It's to do with last night.

CONSTANCE. Don't worry. I'm not upset. I'm not angry. Would you like some coffee?

MARTIN. Not particularly.

CONSTANCE. Daphne dear, make an extra cup.

DAPHNE. Very good Madam.

(DAPHNE goes off into the apartment.)

CONSTANCE. Would you care to sit down?
MARTIN. No, I don't think so. Thank you.
CONSTANCE. Sure? Well you don't mind if I do.

She sits in the corner of the sofa, leaving plenty of space for him. He doesn't sit.)

MARTIN. I hope I didn't overstep the mark last night. It's not the sort of thing I usually do—or do at all, come to that.

CONSTANCE. To be honest, it wasn't exactly an every-day event for me either. I could count how many times I've had someone serenade me, with an orchestra, on the fingers of one hand. A badly mutilated hand at that.

MARTIN. I'm sorry. Strauss isn't everyone's cup of tea. An acquired taste.

CONSTANCE. Well, I'm sure if other people can acquire it, I can—what was it called?

MARTIN. Arabella.

CONSTANCE. Oh. Perhaps he'll write something else.

MARTIN. He has. He did. "Rosenkavalier."

CONSTANCE. Oh yes! Oh , I know that. The Knight who brings the rose. Rather an obvious sort of thing to do.

MARTIN. I suppose it was. I'm sorry.

CONSTANCE. *(Sees the orchid.)* Oh no! I don't mean you, I loved the orchid. Oh—I haven't even put it in the water! Daphne! Daphne come here a moment. *(To MARTIN.)* Unfor-givable of me. *(Enter DAPHNE from the apartment. To DAPHNE.)* This poor plant'll be dead if we don't give it a drink.

(CONSTANCE hands it to DAPHNE.)

DAPHNE. One more for coffee?

(DAPHNE enters with the orchid.)

CONSTANCE. Well now then about last night—

MARTIN. Miss Beaumont, please. What's past is past. I made a fool of myself last night and now let's forget it. Let's forget the serenade, let's forget the champagne and the caviar—

CONSTANCE. Oh, no.

MARTIN. Let's forget the music and the orchid.

CONSTANCE. Please, I—

MARTIN. And let's forget I said I loved you.

CONSTANCE. Why?

MARTIN. Because I don't.

CONSTANCE. You might.

MARTIN. No. I promised myself to another woman.

CONSTANCE. When?

MARTIN. About half-past seven this morning. I rang up Mrs. Foster-Buller. She's expecting me at six o'clock. We're going to see Ariadne on Naxos.

CONSTANCE. You're flying out?

MARTIN. It's another opera.

CONSTANCE. *(With horror.)* Mrs. Foster-Buller! Martin, listen to me. You could be making a terrible mistake. Sit down.

MARTIN. I'd rather not.

CONSTANCE. Sit down, sit!! *(MARTIN sits.)* She's a worthy woman, Martin. She has many fine qualities but I couldn't put my hand on my heart and say she's the ideal soul-mate for you.

MARTIN. Do you know, after Id' poured out my heart to her and she'd said she fully understood, I just felt I'd come to the end of a long journey. And her voice! Have you noticed her voice?

CONSTANCE. Yes! It's awful.

MARTIN. No it isn't. It's strong. It's got authority. It sends a shiver through you. It makes me tingle.

CONSTANCE. It's dreadful.

MARTIN. You're the only one who thinks so.

CONSTANCE. No I'm not. Daphne agrees—where's Daphne? Daphne?!! Where are you? *(Enter DAPHNE with a tray of coffee. The orchid is in a bowl on the tray.)* Haven't we always said what an atrocious voice Mrs. Foster-Buller's got?

DAPHNE. Have we?

CONSTANCE. Well let's say it now anyway. *(To MAR-TIN.)* There, she agrees with me. *(To DAPHNE.)* This dear unfortunate man has made up his mind to throw in his lot with the Buller woman.

DAPHNE. You haven't?

MARTIN. *(Gives DAPHNE a wink.)* I have.

CONSTANCE. Brain fever. On the rebound.

MARTIN. She's a thoroughly good sort. A first-class cook, housekeeper. She's up with the lark.

CONSTANCE. She must have been up this morning. He rang her at seven thirty.

MARTIN. She'd been up since six. To milk the goats.

CONSTANCE. She'll have you doing that. Out there in the cold grey dawn.

MARTIN. Oh no. They live in the kitchen.

DAPHNE. In the kitchen?

MARTIN. It's charming really. She gets on awfully well with animals.

CONSTANCE. Are you an animal lover?

MARTIN. Not up 'til now, I hadn't really thought about it. But that's going to be the wonderful thing about Marigold. That's her name you know.

CONSTANCE. No it isn't, it's Elizabeth.

MARTIN. Ah, yes—no, I mean Marigold's her pet name, for very close friends. We should get on like a house on fire. She loves the idea of ham radio. And she wants to know everything about computers.

CONSTANCE. Well so do I! Don't we all?

MARTIN. Thanks for the coffee. Must dash. Got to catch the next fast train to Reading—*(Backing out.)* Miss Pardoe, Miss Beaumont.

CONSTANCE. Wait, wait! Martin!

MARTIN. Oh, one thing, you're the sort of people who'd

know. Can you get rings altered?

CONSTANCE. The setting?

MARTIN. No, the size. The one I bought for you won't fit her I would think. She's much bigger in the—the—er—

(MARTIN is gesturing as if to say 'in the bosom department.')

DAPHNE. Fingers?

MARTIN. Yes fingers. Well, wish me luck. Do you know if you'd told me two days ago that I'd be taking the plunge with a vicar's widow I'd have said you were off your chump. Isn't it funny what love can do?

CONSTANCE. Stop! I beg you. On bended knee, don't do it!!

MARTIN. What?

CONSTANCE. Don't do it!!

MARTIN. I can't believe my ears! Miss Beaumont of the Beaumont Bureau stopping trade? This is what you're after isn't it? One Client pairing off with another?

CONSTANCE. She'll swamp you! She'll smother you.

MARTIN. Yes! She said she would. She made it sound rather exciting.

CONSTANCE. You'll just be another goat!

MARTIN. I can't think why you're being so rude about Marigold. She's *tremendously* nice.

CONSTANCE. Nice? She's not nice at all. They might have made Henry a bishop if it hadn't been for her. The Dean of Westminster told me that personally.

DAPHNE. I didn't know you knew the Dean.

CONSTANCE. You see Martin, I'm not just in this business for money. Sometimes one has to say "enough"!! The Bureau doesn't want to put its name to misalliances that could've been avoided.

MARTIN. Well, this is a pretty kettle of fish, I must say. I'm committed to this woman, a woman recommended by you. How am I supposed to disentangle myself without giving dreadful offence?

CONSTANCE. We have a formal letter for these tricky occasions, don't we Daphne?

DAPHNE. Yes.

MARTIN. Oh, good.

(DAPHNE goes towards her desk.)

CONSTANCE. *(Deliberately.)* They're in the other room Daphne!

DAPHNE. Oh are they?

CONSTANCE. Yes. Hunt around for a bit.

(DAPHNE goes into the apartment.)

MARTIN. Well, here I am all dressed and no-where to go. No-where to go.

CONSTANCE. *(Wrestling with herself.)* You might—er— you could come to me.

MARTIN. *(Incredulous.)* Come to you? To you?

CONSTANCE. *(Hastily.)* Of course if you don't want to, forget I ever said such a thing.

MARTIN. Oh gosh, I wish I'd known. If only you'd said something before. I've spent half the night erasing you from my memory.

CONSTANCE. Don't make it worse! (There is a knock at the door.) Oh God. Come in.

(MRS. FOSTER-BULLER breezes in.)

MRS. FOSTER-BULLER. I'm dying to tell you—*(Stops.)* Oh, you've got someone with you. Oh it's Mr. Whittaker.

CONSTANCE. Oh, you don't have to be so formal "Mari-gold."

MRS. FOSTER-BULLER. *(Puzzled.)* Marigold?

CONSTANCE. I know you two have been getting a bit

pally on the telephone.

MRS. FOSTER-BULLER. What are you talking about? I've never spoken to him on the 'phone.

CONSTANCE. Oh, it's so transparent. You though you'd poached him. Well now I've poached him back. Martin, tell her I know everything.

MARTIN. Er— why don't I make some more coffee?

(DAPHNE enters with coffee.)

DAPHNE. Don't worry, that's exactly what I've done.

CONSTANCE. *(To MRS. FOSTER-BULLER.)* Who's the Judas now? Who's the Jezabel?

MRS. FOSTER-BULLER. Is this woman possessed or what?

CONSTANCE. I'll tell you who's possessed. *(Points to MARTIN.)* It's him thanks to your wiles. He thinks he's in love with you.

MRS. FOSTER-BULLER. Is this true Mr. Whittaker?

MARTIN. Madly.

MRS. FOSTER-BULLER. Then it's a pity you didn't tell me sooner. I'm very sorry for you, but I'm spoken for. You can strike me off your list again.

DAPHNE. Well, that's good news, isn't it Constance?

CONSTANCE. I'm not sure, I'm lost.

MRS. FOSTER-BULLER. It happened yesterday, on the train back to Reading. It braked suddenly going through Twyford, and I banged into a Canon. Our hands touched, it was history repeating itself. No thanks to you.

DAPHNE. Lovely. It does our hearts good to hear of stories like that though I don't think we can offer a refund.

MRS. FOSTER-BULLER. I'm in a very generous mood. I've been in one ever since I met Canon Ralph Spottiswood.

(MRS. FOSTER-BULLER goes to exit.)

DAPHNE. A widower?

MRS. FOSTER-BULLER. No, the dear man's never been married before. I'll make him regret it.

(MRS. FOSTER-BULLER exits.)

CONSTANCE. *(Rounding on MARTIN.)* If you ever set foot in this building again, with your dreadful lies, I shall have you arrested.

MARTIN. All's fair in love and war, you know.

CONSTANCE. Just where does love come into this?

MARTIN. It comes in as soon as the war is over, and I'm sue-ing for peace.

CONSTANCE. I'm sue-ing for trespass.

MARTIN. You can't. I was invited in.

CONSTANCE. *(Picking up the 'phone.)* Is it still "999", Daphne?

DAPHNE. You can say it was domestic violence, but there is a snag to that.

CONSTANCE. What?

DAPHNE. You'll have to marry him first.

CONSTANCE. Marry him?

MARTIN. I don't expect an answer right away. Tonight'll do at dinner. I'll call for you at seven.

CONSTANCE. I'm not eating any dinner of yours.

MARTIN. It won't be mine, it'll be the Ivy's. After the theatre—

CONSTANCE. Oh, we're going to the theatre are we?

MARTIN. Yes. Another musical feast for you.

CONSTANCE. Not 'Rosenkavalier.'

MARTIN. Not 'Rosenkavalier.'

CONSTANCE. What then?

MARTIN. 'Me and My Girl.'

(MARTIN exits. CONSTANCE appears to be unmoved.)

CONSTANCE. *(Replaces the receiver.)* Good heavens, look at the time. I should have made twenty calls by now. *(She goes to her desk and sits behind it.)* Oh by the way, someone rang for you earlier.

DAPHNE. Who?

CONSTANCE. I can't remember. I expect they'll ring again. Take off your coat. There are these letters for you to type. *(Hands them to DAPHNE.)* Did you get any stamps yesterday?

DAPHNE. Yes.

(DAPHNE goes to her desk and prepares to type.)

CONSTANCE. *(Starts to open a letter and glances at the postmark.)* "Wensleydale." Do we know anyone in Wensleydale?

DAPHNE. No.

CONSTANCE. Our fame is spreading. *(She takes out the letter and reads—)* "Dear Miss Beaumont, I am a—

(CONSTANCE becomes distracted and stares into space.)

DAPHNE. What is it?

CONSTANCE. Do you know Daphne, mine's a lot better looking than yours.

(DAPHNE gives a look of surprise as—
The Curtain Falls.) .

END OF PLAY

PROPERTY LIST

ACT I

Telephone/Answering machine
Desk Computer
Typewriter
Box with files in it
Vase of flowers
Pen in holder
Blotter
Desk Diary
A folding screen about four feet high
Half a dozen letters
A cup and saucer
Telephone on Constance's desk
Brief case with tools—screwdriver etc.
A floppy disc
Cafe Filter
Tray
Cup and Saucer
Computer "mouse"
A pair of sunglasses
An application form
A check book

ACT II

A portable tape recorder
Letter
Bunches of flowers
Check
Handbag
Food hamper containing:
        Champagne
        Champagne glasses

Smoked salmon and caviar
Orchid in a cellophane packet
Two plates and cutlery
An empty milk bottle
A book
Handbag
Coffee cups
Letter

BASIC GROUND PLAN

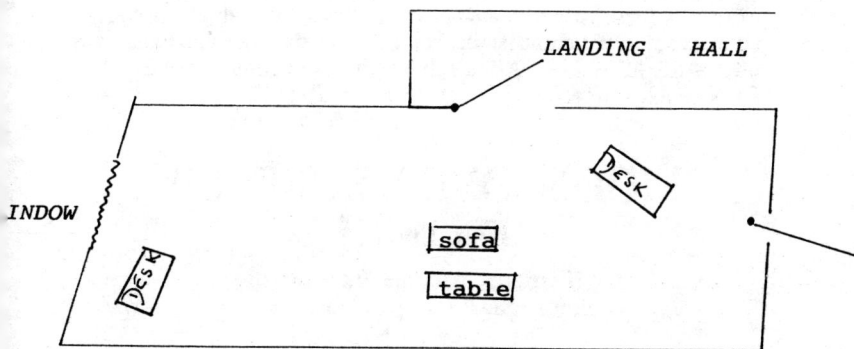

LANDING   HALL

INDOW

Desk

Desk

sofa

table

AUDIENCE

DEATH DEFYING ACTS
David Mamet • Elaine May • Woody Allen

This Off-Broadway hit features comedies by three masters of the genre. David Mamet's brilliant twenty-minute play INTERVIEW is a mystifying interrogation of a sleazy lawyer. In HOTLINE, a wildly funny forty-minute piece by Elaine May, a woman caller on a suicide hotline overwhelms a novice counselor. A psychiatrist has discovered that her husband is unfaithful in Woody Allen's hilarious hour-long second act, CENTRAL PARK WEST. 2 m., 3 f. (#6201)

MOON OVER BUFFALO
Ken Ludwig

A theatre in Buffalo in 1953 is the setting for this hilarious backstage farce by the author of LEND ME A TENOR. Carol Burnett and Philip Bosco starred on Broadway as married thespians to whom fate gives one more shot at stardom during a madcap matinee performance of PRIVATE LIVES - or is it CYRANO DE BERGERAC? 4 m., 4 f. (#17)

Samuel French, Inc.
SERVING THE THEATRICAL COMMUNITY SINCE 1830

Other Publications for Your Interest

NOISES OFF
(LITTLE THEATRE—FARCE)

By MICHAEL FRAYN

5 men, 4 women—2 Interiors

This wonderful Broadway smash hit is "a farce about farce, taking the clichés of the genre and shaking them inventively through a series of kaleidoscopic patterns. Never missing a trick, it has as its first act a pastiche of traditional farce; as its second, a contemporary variant on the formula; as its third, an elaborate undermining of it. The play opens with a touring company dress-rehearsing 'Nothing On', a conventional farce. Mixing mockery and homage, Frayn heaps into this play-within-a-play a hilarious melee of stock characters and situations. Caricatures—cheery char, outraged wife and squeaky blonde—stampede in and out of doors. Voices rise and trousers fall . . . a farce that makes you think as well as laugh."—London Times Literary Supplement. ". . . as side-splitting a farce as I have seen. Ever? *Ever.*"—John Simon, NY Magazine. "The term 'hilarious' must have been coined in the expectation that something on the order of this farce-within-a-farce would eventually come along to justify it."—N.Y. Daily News. "Pure fun."—N.Y. Post. "A joyous and loving reminder that the theatre really does go on, even when the show falls apart."—N.Y. Times.   (#16052)

THE REAL THING
(ADVANCED GROUPS—COMEDY)

By TOM STOPPARD

4 men, 3 women—Various settings

The effervescent Mr. Stoppard has never been more intellectually—and *emotionally*—engaging than in this "backstage" comedy about a famous playwright named Henry Boot whose second wife, played on Broadway to great acclaim by Glenn Close (who won the Tony Award), is trying to merge "worthy causes" (generally a euphemism for left-wing politics) with her art as an actress. She has met a "political prisoner" named Brodie who has been jailed for radical thuggery, and who has written an inept play about how property is theft, about how the State stifles the Rights of The Individual, etc., etc., etc. Henry's wife wants him to make the play work theatrically, which he does after much soul-searching. Eventually, though, he is able to convince his wife that Brodie is emphatically *not* a victim of political repression. He is, in fact, a *thug*. Famed British actor Jeremy Irons triumphed in the Broadway production (Tony Award), which was directed to perfection by none other than Mike Nichols (Tony Award). "So densely and entertainingly packed with wit, ideas and feelings that one visit just won't do . . . Tom Stoppard's most moving play and the most bracing play anyone has written about love and marriage in years."—N.Y. Times. "Shimmering, dazzling theatre, a play of uncommon wit and intelligence which not only thoroughly delights but challenges and illuminates our lives."—WCBS-TV. 1984 Tony Award-Best Play.   (#941)

Other Publications for Your Interest

I'M NOT RAPPAPORT
(LITTLE THEATRE—COMEDY)
By HERB GARDNER

5 men, 2 women—Exterior

Just when we thought there would never be another joyous, laugh-filled evening on Broadway, along came this delightful play to restore our faith in the Great White Way. If you thought *A Thousand Clowns* was wonderful, wait til you take a look at *I'm Not Rappaport!* Set in a secluded spot in New York's Central Park, the play is about two octogenarians determined to fight off all attempts to put them out to pasture. Talk about an odd couple! Nat is a lifelong radical determined to fight injustice (real or imagined) who is also something of a spinner of fantasies. He has a delightful repertoire of eccentric personas, which makes the role an actor's dream. The other half of this unlikely partnership is Midge, a Black apartment super who spends his days in the park hiding out from tenants, who want him to retire. "Rambunctiously funny."—N.Y. Post. "A warm and entertaining evening."—W.W. Daily. **Tony Award Winner, Best Play 1986. Posters.**

(#11071)

CROSSING DELANCEY
(LITTLE THEATRE—COMEDY)
By SUSAN SANDLER

2 men, 3 women—Comb. Interior/Exterior.

Isabel is a young Jewish woman who lives alone and works in a NYC bookshop. When she is not pining after a handsome author who is one of her best customers, she is visiting her grandmother—who lives by herself in the "old neighborhood", Manhattan's Lower East Side. Isabel is in no hurry to get married, which worries her grandmother. The delightfully nosey old lady hires an old friend who is—can you believe this in the 1980's?—a matchmaker. Bubbie and the matchmaker come up with a Good Catch for their Isabel—Sam, a young pickle vendor. Same is no *schlemiel*, though. He likes Isabel; but he knows he is going to have to woo her, which he proceeds to do. When Isabel realizes what a cad the author is, and what a really nice man Sam is, she begins to respond; and the end of the play is really a beginning, ripe with possibilities for Isabel and "An amusing interlude for theatregoers who may have thought that simple romance and sentimentality had long since been relegated to television sitcoms...tells its unpretentious story believeably, rarely trying to make its gag lines, of which there are many, upstage its narration or outshine its heart."—N.Y. Times. "A warm and loving drama...a welcome addition to the growing body of Jewish dramatic work in this country."—Jewish Post and Opinion.

(#5739)